Hoping for Spring

BISHOP KAY WARD

Interprovincial Board of Communication
Moravian Church in North America

Hoping for Spring

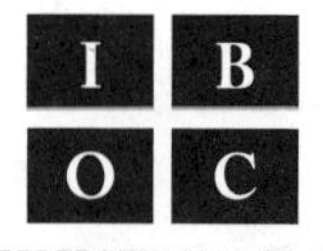

INTERPROVINCIAL BOARD
OF COMMUNICATION

Moravian Church in North America
PO Box 1245, 1021 Center Street
Bethlehem, Pennsylvania, 18016-1245
800.732.0591
www.moravian.org

Book design: Sandy Fay,
Laughing Horse Graphics Inc., Doylestown, Pennsylvania

Front cover illustration: © Debra Jane Carey
www.interactionart.com
Back cover photo: Christmas City Studio, Bethlehem, Pennsylvania.
Used by permission.

ISBN: 978-1-933571-19-5

Printed in the United States of America.

DEDICATION

For Milo who shares his life and faith with complete joy.

For family that we would choose to be best friends.

For best friends that always feel like family.

Dear Lord, we are thankful.

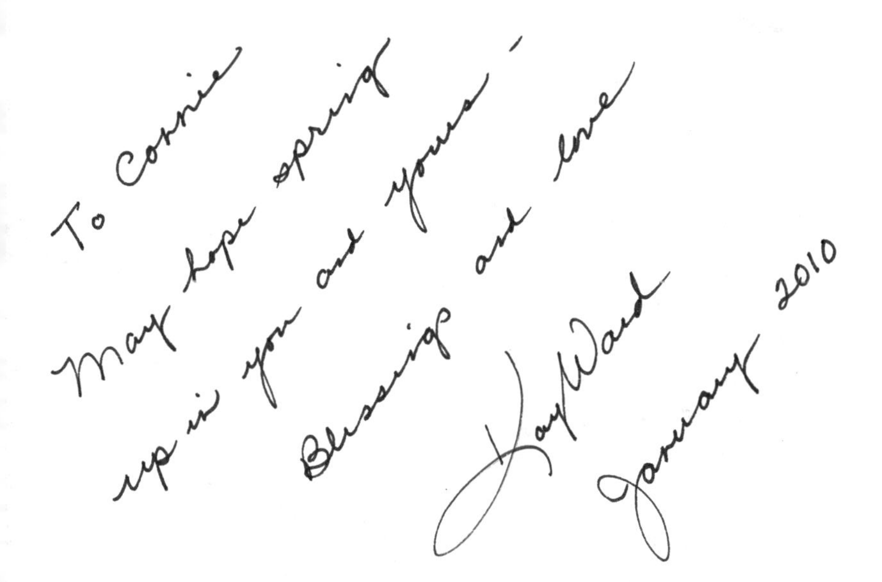

FOREWORD

After a cold Wisconsin winter, there is nothing that speaks of spring more than spring flowers. But I am not talking about the sweet miniatures that sleep under the ice and snow and push themselves up at the very first warmth of the sun. Put your trust in those small beauties and you will find yourself up to your knees in an April snowstorm!

Put your trust in a sure sign of spring in Wisconsin — the blooming of the trillium. The trillium is featured on the cover of this book. See page ix for more about this beautiful woods flower.

Please allow me to publicly thank my cousin Trish for her generous gift of artwork and botanical information. (She uses Debra Jane Carey professionally.) Ken and Trish have been in the process of this book, providing a warm place in January to write and dream and the warmth of their hearts the rest of the year.

So when we see the first trillium, we get the porches cleaned off and know that spring will be coming soon.

The first trillium gives us hope — a rising in the spirit — a looking ahead to the promise of sunny days.

This book is about that kind of hope, of living with expectancy, of anticipating the turning of the pages —

the turning of the pages of the books, magazines, and journals we hold in our hands,

the turning of the pages of the calendar, offering a fresh new month,

the turning of the pages of our lives, hoping for spring.

About the Illustrator

Debra Jane Carey

Botanical illustration is a balance between the realistic rendering of a plant, and the stylistic interpretation of the artist.

Debra Jane Carey is an internationally recognized and award-winning artist who brings nature alive by spotlighting in breathtaking detail the magic of plants and animals.

The Artist-Illustrator joined the University of Illinois Master Gardener Program in 1993 where she trained in botany and entomology.

Carey achieved her Certificate in Botanical Art & Illustration in 1998. Her art embodies her fine draftsmanship and a thorough understanding of the subject matter. In 2002, Carey taught research, history, and techniques of botanical illustration at Ringling School of Art and Design. The compilation of this course is detailed in the book, "Ten Steps: A Course in Botanical Art & Illustration," Vol. III O.M. Briada 2005.

Most recently Ms. Carey has further extended her education by obtaining a Certificate from The Sarasota School of Faux & Architectural Finishes. Combining her expertise with these unique products and techniques is providing a fresh approach to her illustrative wall murals.

Carey exhibits nationally and locally. She has collaborated with Selby

Botanical Gardens in Sarasota, Florida, to create poster artwork that won the "education award" during the American Orchid Society Florida tour.

Her products are sold at nature stores nationwide.

<www.interactionart.com>

The Story of White Trillium

White Trillium

Trillium grandiflorum (Michx.) Salsb., 1805 Liliaceae North America

The genus trillium seems to be a derived word from the Swedish word, trilling, relating to the three leaves and petals. Trillium is distributed in North America, the Himalayas, and East Asia. In North America, the Mississippi River valley is the western boundary with the plant species extending from Canada to Alabama and Georgia.

Trillium are long-lived perennials of rich deciduous upland forests. Oak, maple, and beech help make up this habitat. The rich, leaf-littered soil brings a wealth of nutrients to the life of the trillium.

A single rootstock forms dense colonies. The bloom is odorless with three overlapping petals that form a funnel shape. There are variations in color during flowering, opening vibrant white then fading to pink. Seeds require two years to germinate and take 7-10 years to reach flowering.

This species does not self-pollinate but requires a pollinating host. Bumble bees (*Ceratina dupla* — Little Carpenter Bee) pollinate up to two meters, *Myrmica americana* ants disperse trillium seed short distances, and white-tailed deer (*Odocoileus virginianus*) distribute the seed long distances. There is evidence deer may have been responsible for migrating populations of seed after the last glacial period. Researchers reconstructed the movement of trillium using leaf samples found throughout the range. Maple and Beech species growing in present day Alabama and Arkansas moved north during the Wisconsin glacial retreat 20,000 years ago.

There are no known cultivated trillium. This means garden populations only come from wild seed or root stock which causes current conservation concern. Wild collecting, habitat destruction, and grazing are major factors attributed to population decline, but nature has a way of balancing the scale, with animals and ants carrying and dispersing the seed and creating new colonies of the trillium for people to enjoy.

Table Of Contents

First Things First

For those of you who have read *Of Seasons and Sparrows* and *Heading Home*, (bless you), I will start with a word about how this book has come about. This is the first collection I have written since I retired. Shortly after sending *Heading Home* to press, I received word the column I had been writing once a month, for 10 years, had been discontinued. I no longer had a monthly deadline. I no longer had a target of 500 words. I no longer had to write for a general, newspaper reading audience – those anonymous folks who might read the article while drinking their morning coffee. I was set free.

I could write amok with few restraints but as you will see, I haven't written amok very far. That is because I am an essayist. I didn't know I was an essayist until I went to my first and only writing conference.

As I was picking out workshops to attend, I saw one that read, *Shaping an Essay* by Brian Doyle. Essays can be, in Doyle's words, "a superb and lovely ocean of ink." In this session, he offers his thoughts on catching essays out of the air, hearing the way they begin, and grappling with their serpentine allure, along with further ruminations on why the essay is the greatest written form of all. To be honest, nothing else caught my eye in that time slot so I went. I fell in love with Brian Doyle, an Irish essayist, poet, and professor of creative writing. As he talked about the different aims of writing poems, novels, and essays, I understood myself to be an essayist. Being an essayist means I like to write 500 words (more or less) about almost anything. Actually, I can write 500 words about nothing — no plot, no characters (well, maybe a couple), and no great surprise endings or morals of the story.

This book is different in another way — I have divided the book into 12 sections, one for each month. The first chapter of each month is not my typical essay — it is more an introduction to that particular month. It will include some words about the month as I experience it in Wisconsin, a short story from the Bible, a few recipes, and several short essays of my own.

I am conscious that most of my readers will be people of faith. So, in this book, instead of using a verse of scripture at the beginning of each chapter, I have chosen 12 of my favorite biblical short stories. They stand on their own but some of you might want to put the story in its context by reading verses before and after the short story. Living with a text over time is always an enlightening practice for me so you might try reading it over and over as you read through the month.

I have closed with prayers of gratitude, pure and simple. I trust that you will want to add your own prayers of thanksgiving if you are using this book in a devotional way.

Lastly, with some unease, I have included two of my own short stories from my "Frances" series. It is easy for me to share essays with you but a short story is a very different matter — be gentle as you read.

Welcome to book three — *Hoping for Spring* — may you be blessed in the reading as I have been blessed in the writing.

Thank you, Holy God, for wonderful writers like Brian Doyle, time to write 500 words or less, stories of all kinds, and the biblical word. Amen.

January

The month of new pages — a whole new year
Hanging up new calendars — putting Christmas away
New resolve to feed the birds, lose some weight
Cold and crisp — crunchy snow
January is silver and white on a good day
Black and gray on a bad
It is a month of sharp edges

Jesus Cleanses Ten Lepers — Luke 17:11-19

On the way to Jerusalem, Jesus was going through the region between Samaria and Galilee. As he entered a village, ten lepers approached him. Keeping their distance, they called out, saying, "Jesus, Master, have mercy on us!" When he saw them, he said to them, "Go and show yourselves to the priests." And as they went, they were made clean. Then one of them, when he saw that he was healed, turned back, praising God with a loud voice. He prostrated himself at Jesus' feet and thanked him. And he was a Samaritan. Then Jesus asked, "Were not ten made clean? But the other nine, where are they? Was none of them found to return and give praise to God except this foreigner?" Then he said to him, "Get up and go on your way; your faith has made you well."

Weight Watchers and Jesus

Speaking of the resolve to lose weight, I am a WW! After many years of avoiding the topic of losing weight or of trying to lose weight on my own, I finally joined Weight Watchers. I made a commitment to it. I liked the leader, I liked the program, and it worked for me. Mostly, I liked the group of people I met with every Tuesday morning — a really important support group who knew how to comfort when I had a bad week, to cheer when I had a good week, and to be still when I didn't want to talk about it. After many, many months, people began to notice that I was losing a bit of weight and I loved telling folks about our leader — about the program — about the dear people who were so crucial to my success. I eagerly looked forward to the next opportunity to share my story — to retell the funny things people said — to proclaim the amazing results of this life-changing experience.

After one of my soapbox witness talks about WW, a wise friend asked me this — "I wonder if you have brought as many people to Jesus as you have to the WW program?" That got my attention in a hurry. And I had to admit, the answer is no. I probably haven't brought as many people to Jesus as I have to WW. What a sad commentary. Having a life in Christ has been life-changing for me — much more life-changing than Weight Watchers. But maybe people don't notice that change in me anymore. They should be able to tell by watching how I live that I serve a risen Savior.

January is a good month to think about this and make another resolve.

Thank you, Holy God, for new beginnings, people who understand, healthy food to eat, and a Savior who can change our lives. Amen.

Clearing The Windshield

I sit inside our very cold car. My teeth are chattering. I can see my breath in little puffs of white. It's winter in Wisconsin. We have spent a pleasant evening with friends and have come out to the driveway to find our car covered with a coating of ice and snow. And while I am sitting inside, out of the wind in the passenger seat, with the car heater trying its best to warm up, I watch my husband. There he is, outside the car, cleaning off the snow and ice. He starts on the side of the car, brushing off snow that has accumulated on the roof so it doesn't blow off onto the windshield when we start to move. He cleans off the side view window ledges and uses the scraper to get every little bit of ice clinging to the side and back windows. He cleans off the rear brake lights and the license plate and moves around to my side of the car. He cleans the ice off the windows, and my side view mirror until he gets to the front of the car. The snow from the hood is removed and then he begins the meticulous scraping of ice and snow from the windshield. Then each windshield wiper is pulled out and away from the windshield as he carefully removes each little piece of ice that may be clinging to the rubber of the wiper blade.

By this time, the car is warming up and we are ready to safely head for home. I tell this story only because I have been known to use copious amounts of washer fluid with the windshield wiper to try and clean a spot to see out of to drive. It doesn't work very well and I get pink cleaner fluid all over the ice and snow on the front of the car but I can see to drive through a tiny spot. It's quick and I'm out of the cold.

This attention to detail is just one of the things I love about my husband. For 45 years, I have arrived home safely in one blizzard after another because of the care my husband has taken to make sure the windshields were clear and safe. The attention to detail is also evident in the fact that every winter morning, he gets up and prepares the wood stove. He empties the ashes into a metal bucket, sprays the glass door with window cleaner, dips a crumpled up newspaper in the ashes and shines the glass. Then he sets the fire with more crumpled up newspaper, kindling, and some soft wood logs and lights the fire to get our home toasty warm.

He makes sure the salt is in the water softener, bird seed in the birdfeeders, and washes the dishes when I cook. And every night before we turn in, he checks the doors to see that they are all locked and pats the large flashlight he has beside the bed for emergencies.

These are small things perhaps but I don't think I have ever said thank you. I guess that is why I wrote this story. I receive very good care. Thank you, Aden.

Thank you, Holy God, for wood stoves on a cold day, a husband who cares, shelter from the storm, and safe travels. Amen.

Light In The Woods

For city folks, our cabin in the woods is just too dark. No street lights, no car lights, no ambient light of any kind, so when we have guests, we turn on night lights in many parts of the house so they can navigate to the bathrooms safely when they get up in the middle of the night. Many years ago when our young nephew was visiting us, he staggered downstairs for breakfast looking like he had had a hard night. I asked him how he had slept. He said, "Aunt Kay, I didn't sleep at all. It was so dark, I couldn't tell if I had my eyes open or closed."

Aden and I know our way around in the dark but Aden is a man who seems to have transparent eyelids so even the darkest night isn't dark enough for him. He notices the lights from the smoke alarms, from the digital clock, and all the red and green and white lights from our various appliances in the kitchen. When the moon is full in a cloudless sky, my husband thinks we should have darkening shades for our bedroom. I tell him that when I shut my eyes, the lights go out. Apparently, his don't work that way.

All of this is to say our woods can be very dark at night, which is why I love winter in the woods. When the leaves are off the trees, I can't wait for the first time I wake up in the middle of the night and see the "stars in the trees." I usually wake Aden up and say, "The stars are back in the trees." He groans and rolls over. I mentioned the "stars in the trees" phenomenon to my friend who teaches astronomy and she said, "The winter sky is different. The cold weather clears up the atmosphere so you can see stars closer to the horizon." And of course, I could tell that we can see the stars because the branches are bare. The stars in the trees look exactly like Christmas trees, with tiny white lights attached to every branch, except these are placed perfectly and don't need batteries.

Each winter since we have moved to the woods, as soon as the leaves are gone, I look forward to another woods phenomenon, seeing the "light" in the woods. I can see it through our window when I lie in bed. There it is, twinkling in the night, especially bright on starless, moonless nights. It must be someone's yard light, way through the woods. I even tried to figure out whose light it was by driving down the back road, trying to imagine which farm it might be but I couldn't figure it out. But it made me feel good to know my unknown neighbors were there.

But this winter, in the very first few dark days of November, I noticed that the light was gone. Not only did I not know whose light it was to begin with, now I didn't know what happened to it. Did the people move? Is the farm empty? Did the light burn out and no one has bothered to replace it? Was it sold to folks who don't see the need for a yard light? Maybe new people moved in who have transparent eyelids too? I don't know what happened, but I know that I do miss the assurance of that twinkly light on a dark night in our woods. I hope everything is OK.

Thank you, Holy God, for light on a moonless night, neighbors I know and those I don't, the wonder of a full moon, and the light of Jesus Christ in a dark world. Amen.

Saturday Afternoon In The ER

If one is a people watcher, this is the place for it. It's 2:00 pm and I've been here for an hour, waiting for a friend. I've knit several inches on the sock I always have with me. Since then, I have just been watching. They come into this hospital on a Saturday from their weekend lives. Three tall, muscular, young men have come out of the treatment area in wheelchairs or crutches. I hope they were having fun — now they carry prescriptions for pain-killers — they won't be having much fun the rest of the weekend. A couple comes in, the man straight from yard work. He has dirt on his knees and somthing in his eye, his wife says later, as she waits beside me in the waiting area. Actually, she says, he got something in his eye earlier, before lunch and she washed out his eye and it looked fine to her. But he is such a worrier she says, so he insisted on coming in to have it checked. He's kind of a baby about these things she says.

A young woman brings in her toddler in a wheelchair. The chair is way too big for the little girl. She explains to the nurse in bits of Spanish and English that her little girl has hurt her leg. The little girl, about three I'd guess, is bouncing up and down in the wheelchair. I watch as her mother tries to keep her in the chair, then transfers her to a waiting room chair, where the little girl scrambles up on her feet and looks over the top of the high backed chair. She giggles and teases with her mother and it's hard to believe that she is seriously hurt, but what do I know?

All of a sudden, after a rather quiet time, things pick up. A young woman wheels in her mother. She has fallen and seems confused. About the same time, the ambulance arrives and two EMTs bring in an elderly woman in a wheelchair who has had some kind of accident. Waiting at the window, a mother hugs her young daughter who has had flu-like symptoms for four days. It's noisy and busy as people jockey for position to check in.

The door opens again and a man in a dark gray windbreaker steps in. He grabs hold of the sign that is standing just outside the door. It says, "Please wait here to be registered." His voice is quiet but it pierces through the din. He says, "I'm having chest pains. My cardiologist told me to come." Still holding on to the sign, he turns and I can see his face. I've heard people say that someone looked gray. This man's face is gray — a few shades lighter than his jacket. The nurse asks him if he has ever had problems with his heart. (She clearly didn't hear him say that his cardiologist had told him to come in.) He said that he has had four heart attacks. Four heart attacks? I wanted to jump out of my seat and start screaming, "This man is having a heart attack! Do something!" But I restrained myself and the triage nurse grabbed a wheelchair and said, "Let's get him back in there to see someone." And they did. I breathed a sigh of relief. Just an ordinary Saturday and for that man and for any of us, it could become THE Saturday, the last Saturday. I hope it wasn't for this man. He seemed nice. I said a prayer.

Thank you, Holy God, for the kindness of those who care for us, medical skills, the ability of our bodies to heal, and the saving power of Jesus Christ. Amen.

February

Seduced by the warmth of valentines
We put promise in the thawing
Only to be clobbered by winter again
February is a month of red and white
Lace and ribbon and roses
Chocolate cake and red food
A perfect month for romance
Because it's too cold to do anything else

The Good Samaritan — Luke 10:29b-37

He asked Jesus, "And who is my neighbor?" Jesus replied, "A man was going down from Jerusalem to Jericho, and fell into the hands of robbers, who stripped him, beat him, and went away, leaving him half dead. Now by chance a priest was going down that road; and when he saw him, he passed by on the other side. So likewise a Levite, when he came to the place and saw him, passed by on the other side. But a Samaritan while traveling came near him; and when he saw him, he was moved with pity. He went to him and bandaged his wounds, having poured oil and wine on them. Then he put him on his own animal, brought him to an inn, and took care of him. The next day he took out two denarii, gave them to the innkeeper, and said, 'Take care of him; and when I come back, I will repay you whatever more you spend.' Which of these three, do you think, was a neighbor to the man who fell into the hands of the robbers?" He said, "The one who showed him mercy." Jesus said to him, "Go and do likewise."

I started making granola in the early 1970s when I was in my earth mother phase. I have just never stopped making it and our family fondly calls it "chicken feed." Our daughter likes to eat the chunks that stick together and my sister likes it without milk but most of the rest of us eat it in the usual cereal way. It is hearty and filling and has made my husband the man he is today. It is a perfect way to start a cold day in February or any other month for that matter.

I have repeated this recipe over and over in response to late night telephone calls and emails. Actually, this is the recipe that made me think I should include some recipes in this third book.

Kay Ward's Granola (aka Chicken Feed)

1 large box of regular oatmeal (42 ounces)
1 – 1½ cups of coconut
½ cup wheat germ
1 cup chopped pecans
1 cup canola oil
1 cup honey

Mix the dry ingredients together in a large bowl and then add the oil and honey. If you are of a delicate nature, you can use a spoon. I use my hands.

Layer the granola on cookie sheets, not too thick, and bake in a 350 degree oven for 15 minutes. While it is still hot, remove and put in a storage container. I usually use a big glass jar but you can use anything airtight.

Thank you, Holy God, for neighbors who will stop and help, mushy valentines, hearty breakfasts, and things that last. Amen.

The Music Contest

The cafeteria of the high school is buzzing with activity. Parents sit patiently nursing their cups of coffee and giant sweet rolls. Small clusters of teenagers lean into each other, checking their phrasing on the second verse. Woodwind players walk around sucking their reeds. Tall young men stride proudly in medieval costumes. Official looking adults with clipboards and name tags check schedules and the long manila envelopes they carry. It is the district music contest on a Saturday morning in February. Junior high girls and boys giggle and skitter about with nervous energy. Students have come willingly to test themselves.

We had begun the morning in a large auditorium, just minutes before a large jazz band had been assembled. The music had been loud and staccato, saxes blaring. Now at the grand piano sat an accompanist and standing near the center of the stage were two junior high students. The girl was tall and thin — a shiny brown skirt swirling around her skinny legs. Beside her, at least a head shorter, a young boy stood. She held a flute and he a trumpet. They played "Amazing Grace" in harmony. The sound was as thin as their bodies but the notes were in place and the judge praised them when they finished.

I knew where our high school friend would be performing in solo and ensemble, but on the way to watch him, I stepped into a large classroom to catch another performer who was just beginning. She was a small girl, a freshman in high school in a fancy sheer dress with a flowery hem line. Her thin arms hung at her sides, folding and refolding the fabric of her skirt. Her fingernails were bitten to the quick and painted bright red. Her toes were crammed into summery high heeled sandals, each toe painted dark burgundy. The judge nodded for her to begin. She lifted her head, looked him squarely in the eye and in a clear strong voice said her name and what she was going to sing. She began an art song in German with a quivery soprano voice, as out of her context as anything could be, but she soldiered on. Some high notes were missed but some pierced through, clear and bright. When she missed a phrase or a note, her face clouded up, an eyebrow lifted, or the hands came together in front of her. She finished to flimsy applause and stood still as the judge bent over her paperwork. It must have taken everything she had to either not burst into tears or raise her arms in "Rocky" relief. The judge was kind and professional in her critique.

I was in awe of the courage I had just seen demonstrated. I thought to myself, this is how it starts. It starts by willingly putting yourself to the test, by making yourself perform in front of strangers. This is how it starts but the years will pass quickly and each challenge, met with courage, will lead to the next challenge. And soon, there she will be, standing in her designer pumps and her very expensive red wool suit with the fashionable gold piece of jewelry, as the CEO of her own company — I'll bet she does a great job!

Thank you, Holy God, for music played well or well enough, young people's courage, places to test ourselves, and hope in a flowery dress. Amen.

The Lone Bridesmaid

We were privileged to be spending the Christmas holidays in California with our children, and were staying in the empty apartment of Katie and Travis and Molly. Travis is a Marine stationed in Iraq and Katie and Molly, the bulldog, are in Wisconsin for Christmas. On the nightstand is a picture of Katie and Travis' wedding of almost a year ago, a wedding in which Aden and I were privileged to have a part. Katie and Travis were high school classmates who fell in love at the spring musical, "Annie Get Your Gun." Travis joined the Marines after graduation. Katie worked at a flower shop and began to take college classes. Together, (he always many states or countries away and she at home in Wisconsin) they planned the perfect wedding. Mother, Becky, was sewing all the dresses. Dad, Mel, was building a gazebo for wedding gifts and cards. The wedding was to take place in the performing arts center of the high school. Katie and Travis would take their vows on the same stage where they had sung "There's No Business Like Show Business."

Both Katie and Travis are young people who are rich in friends. Travis had traveled through junior high and senior high school with six very close friends. They would all be in the wedding. Upon graduation, five of the men enlisted in the armed services and one began college. Stints in Iraq and other dangerous assignments threatened the lives of the six men but it was a car accident a few miles from home that took the life of Jason. The group of six was now five!

As the final preparations for the wedding progressed, Katie and Travis chose to have a lighted candle to the right of the stage, to remember Jason. It was subtle but very present as Jason's absence was so present. This is what they wrote in the wedding bulletin: "The candle near the piano is lit as a reminder of our friend and groomsman, Jason Greeno, who passed away in 2006. Although he may not be present to share this day, he is still with us in our hearts." It was a fitting tribute.

Aden and I took our place on stage and watched as the procession formed — five handsome men, four in uniform, one in a tuxedo, waiting to escort the bridesmaids and maid of honor down the long aisle of the auditorium. The men peeled off, each taking the arm of a beautiful young woman dressed in a stunning black gown. And then one young woman stepped out alone. She walked straight and tall and lovely, without an escort. The witness was palpable, as folks caught the meaning. Jason would have been the escort.

There was something very brave and appropriate about the gesture, no grandstanding, no sad stories, just the recognition that friendships cannot easily be replaced. It was recognition that in the midst of all the joy, in the midst of all the celebration, there is always the reality of loss and pain. It doesn't end the joy. In fact, it makes the joy braver. It speaks of hope and courage in the face of anything life can throw us. This couple will do well. They are made of sturdy stuff, wise beyond their years, and already well on the way to knowing what in the world really matters.

Congratulations, Katie and Travis.

Thank you, Holy God, for weddings that begin a new life together, dreams that come true, the value of friendships, and the ability to face all of life. Amen.

With My Own Eyes

I am a very blessed woman. My travels have been a gift and have given me experiences that I will always treasure. In 1995, we traveled to Namibia to visit our daughter who was in the Peace Corps and spent three delicious days in the Etoshe Game Park. One evening at dusk, we sat on a rocky ledge overlooking a large waterhole. The rocky steps were filled with tourists. It was sacred space with the hundred or so spectators sitting quietly, almost silent, waiting. Into the quiet stepped the elephants. They moved leisurely, heading for the water. One by one, the stately animals arrived. And in amidst the adults scampered the baby elephants. They were so tiny that they could stand upright under the bellies of their mothers. They were perfect replicas of the grownups. We held our breath as they circled the water. We exhaled as the last one took her place and then we sat back to watch the choreography as 29 elephants moved around the waterhole. They danced in and out of the water, they drank, they waded, and they circled. As other animals, a rhino, a hyena, a giraffe, approached the hole, the matriarch, a huge female would charge them to protect her tribe. I saw this with my own eyes.

In *Heading Home* I shared the story of standing at the railing of a cruise ship and watching a large research ship sink, watching until all that remained was a small rubber raft. I saw this with my own eyes.

And on a cold February morning, I was just coming awake while Aden splashed water on his face in the bathroom. I heard him say "Kay, look out the bedroom window." I jumped out of bed, looking out at the huge oak tree that stood at the edge of the woods and I couldn't believe what I was seeing. Nestled in the very top of the big oak tree were turkeys, lots of them roosting. We counted them — 23 huge turkeys each settled on a branch way at the top of the tree. It seemed impossible that they could rest there. The branches were too little and they were too big. But rest they did, sleeping snugly on their precarious perches. The sun was just peeking over the garage roof and as the bright light reached the topmost branches, the turkeys began to stir, lifting their heads as they felt the warmth of the sun. They shook their feathers and stretched their necks. The top of the tree slowly woke up and branches shuddered. Morning had broken. We watched, holding our breath, and over the next 15 minutes or so, the big birds, one by one, swooped down to begin their day in the woods. I saw this with my own eyes.

We see turkeys all the time at our bird feeders — we have seen as many as 60 of them out for a stroll in the woods. I have no idea how many times we have missed turkeys roosting in trees near our house. There are wonderful things going on in our woods all the time which we never see. All I know now is that every morning when I wake up, I look up into the oak tree, hoping to see turkeys. I hope I can see them again sometime with my own eyes.

Thank you, Holy God, for animals large and small, travels that make our lives bigger, things we never see, and things that we have seen with our own eyes. Amen.

March

The cruelest month in Wisconsin
Still up to our eyeballs in snow
A quirky Leprechaun kind of month
Against the snow, the goldfinches
Show the hint of greenish yellow
If the sun hits them right
Dirty white snow ringed with edges
Like crusts of brown bread
Green eggs and ham
Mashed potatoes and pancakes too
Green and white — the green is in there
Somewhere — under that snow bank

Jesus Heals Many at Simon's House — Mark 1:29-34

As soon as they left the synagogue, they entered the house of Simon and Andrew, with James and John. Now Simon's mother-in-law was in bed with a fever, and they told him about her at once. He came and took her by the hand and lifted her up. Then the fever left her, and she began to serve them. That evening, at sundown, they brought to him all who were sick or possessed with demons. And the whole city was gathered around the door. And he cured many who were sick with various diseases, and cast out many demons; and he would not permit the demons to speak, because they knew him.

March can be the longest month in Wisconsin, all 31 days of it. The pages are turned slowly. Will spring ever get here, we wonder? It's a good month to think about waiting.

Many years ago, when our youngest daughter was five or six, she brought home some bulbs from her school and we proudly planted them in the back yard. I explained to her that she would have to wait for them to begin to grow. It would take awhile.

I forgot about the bulbs. I was in seminary at the time and I probably forgot about a lot of things but it did occur to me several weeks later that we should be seeing some sign of the bulbs by now. I asked Melly if she had checked on them lately and she assured me that she had been watching them carefully. In fact, she went on to explain, she had been digging them up every day to see if they were growing.

It is hard to wait. I am not good at waiting. I can still remember how long December was when I was a child. Those days until Christmas went by so slowly, dark and cold in Wisconsin. Advent calendars helped but still the days crawled by.

I waited for our wedding. It was over a year after we set the date. I crossed the days off on a long strip of paper. I started at 412 days. It was hard to wait.

But now I can't figure out what happened. After all these years of waiting for things to happen, now the days seem to be speeding by. My mother said this would happen.

Thank you, Holy God, for hints of spring, the lesson of waiting, the possibility of new growth, and the passing of our days. Amen.

Multitude of Sins

It's halfway through Lent and I have come to worship. I am sitting at the foot of the cross. That's not a metaphor. I am literally sitting in a pew just a few feet from the large old weathered, wooden cross that gets hauled into the sanctuary for the Lenten season. What should I be thinking about in Lent? What should I do? We're only halfway through so there is still opportunity to do something to set this time apart. The scripture text from Peter's epistle breaks into my dreaming and demands my attention:

"The end of all things is near: therefore be serious and discipline yourselves for the sake of your prayers. Above all, maintain constant love for one another, for love covers a multitude of sins." (1 Peter 4:7,8)

It is the last phrase that catches my attention. "Love covers a multitude of sins." I will confess that I would not have been able to tell you where you could find that phrase in the scriptures. I wouldn't have been sure that it even came from scripture. But there it was, being read on a Sunday halfway through Lent.

This text is about human relationships. A story comes into my mind. Joan Chittister tells about her childhood in *Living Well.* Joan grew up in a poor family and as a little girl remembers worrying because her father had lost his job. As she was being tucked in bed for the night, she asked her father if they were going to starve to death. Without saying a word, her father picked her up, carried her to the window and pointed across the street to a small grocery store.

"What do you see in front of the store?" he asked. "Windows" she said.

The father replied, "As long as there are windows in grocery stores, my family will not starve." Horrified, the little girl said, "But stealing would be a sin, wouldn't it Daddy?" "When people have nothing to eat, it is not a sin to steal food," he replied.

Love covers a multitude of sins. And those sins may not be what we think they are. It is so easy for us to equate sin with not breaking the rules. Sin may be more about failing to be the person we are called to be, and love has a lot to do with that. But the text for today seems bigger than the human relationships we have. What kind of love could really cover a multitude of sins?

I am curious that Jesus spent so much time with sinners. Jesus could see through those sinners. He could find in them some need of mercy, some opening for change. They readily offered up their failures so that Jesus could make them whole again. I wonder if I could have been so transparent had I lived then. I think I would have been too busy trying to cover up my failures for Jesus to see any need in me. Jesus had the kind of love that could cover a multitude of sins, the kind of love that did cover our sins. That is good news for those of us who sit at the foot of the cross, halfway through Lent.

Thank you, Holy God, for the six weeks of Lent, mercy and the forgiveness of sin, willingness to confess, and for your love that covers a multitude of sins. Amen.

Ironing

I made some new friends and was invited to their house for dinner and conversation. As I arrived, they gave me a tour of their beautiful home. The lower level was a family room with TV and a fireplace, a warm, cozy place where you could see they spent a lot of time. In a prominent place stood an ironing board with neat stacks of clothing and linen waiting to be ironed. I blurted out something stupid like, "Wow, you're a little behind in your ironing."

"Oh," said Mary Ann, "that's what I do in the evenings while we watch TV. I love to iron. I iron everything. It's so satisfying. I love smoothing out the wrinkles after a busy day at work."

I was stunned. I had never heard anyone actually say they loved to iron, but then I come from a long line of folks for whom ironing was a tedious chore. If she had to iron, my mother always gave things "a lick and a promise" which meant just enough to get by. She was also an expert at hanging clothes on the clothesline so perfectly, that the clothes came in sweet smelling and almost wrinkle free. When she bought a dryer, she perfected the timing so that clothes were at their wrinkle free peak and could be hung right up on hangers and taken to the closet. My mother-in-law still irons for her daughters — acts of love surely but I suspect she also doesn't mind ironing. I hate to iron and I have been known to "lose" articles of clothing that require serious ironing and I work very hard to grab the clothes from the dryer at their best.

Which is why you will be able to tell that the following story "Making the Bed" is a made-up story and not autobiographical. It has been edited to fit the format of this book.

Making The Bed — A Frances Story

Frances had taken to ironing a shirt or two of Carl's each afternoon before she began her supper. She laid the sleeve flat out on the ironing board and carefully lined up the seam. She could see the crease she had made the last time she ironed this shirt. It was a button down shirt, white with a thin blue line. Tiny buttons each with four holes, the thread making little "x's," kept the collar looking crisp and also closed the placket on the cuff of the sleeve. Carl was never good at buttoning those tiny buttons so Frances always re-buttoned the collar and sleeve when she finished ironing.

She liked the yoke of his shirts best. They fit so snugly over the end of the ironing board and she could almost feel Carl's strong shoulders as she smoothed the curve of the fabric. As she put the finishing touches on the front of the shirt, she bent down to the board. And there in the steam and heat from the iron came the smell, the smell that made tears well up in her eyes. It was that old familiar masculine smell of her husband almost more familiar to her than her own body smell. She breathed deeply, filling her lungs with the warm fragrant air from the shirt and then hung the shirt up and returned it to the closet where it hung alongside all the rest of Carl's freshly pressed shirts.

This evening, she looked around the kitchen before starting supper, trying to remember what this time used to be like. It alarmed her that she had already begun to forget the little details of an ordinary day. She would be at the sink and the back door would open and Carl would come in from work. He would ask "What's for supper?" He asked the question every night, but he didn't seem to ever listen to her answer. Anything she fixed for him was just fine. He was not a picky eater. The question was just part of the coming home ritual.

He would climb the stairs to wash up and by the time he reentered the kitchen, Frances would have begun her final preparations for the meal. They called it supper. It was eaten at 5:00 pm which seemed to them a good time to eat. They could never understand those folks who ate what they called their evening meal, dinner, long after dark. Carl and Frances ate supper and it consisted of three items, a piece of meat, something starchy (usually potatoes), and a vegetable which to Frances and Carl meant corn, green beans, or peas out of a "Green Giant" can. A pot of tea accompanied the jello or pudding for dessert. Supper was a dependable thing for them both and they took their time drinking their tea.

Now Frances tried to think of three things to fix for supper. It just seemed like too much work to prepare, so as she had so many times in the last few weeks, she opened a can of soup and made a piece of toast. She put on a pot of coffee because the little tea pot was just too full of memories.

In her small tidy kitchen, she watched the news while she ate because it seemed more normal to do that, as if the reason she was not talking to anyone was because she was listening intently to an important late breaking news story, rather than the fact that she was alone at the kitchen table. As she sat down to her simple supper, she told herself she had made it through another day.

The next morning, Frances opened her eyes to a brand new day. She reached out to the far side of the bed and smoothed the sheets expecting to feel them still warm from Carl's exit earlier. They were cold and she was shocked fully awake by the realization that once again Carl had not slept in his usual place. The sheets no longer held the indentation of his body. She reached for his pillow where she could still smell his presence, his hair lotion, and his soap. She held the pillow to her face and imagined him there in his usual place beside her.

Slowly, Frances put his pillow back in its place and sat up on her side of the bed. She let her toes find her slippers and breathed in the morning. Morning was a time of possibilities and right then, Frances was filled with hope, with the potential of a new day. She would do brave things today. She would return her friend's phone call. She would open some of the stack of letters and sympathy cards and maybe even respond to a few.

And perhaps today she would even be brave enough for the big test. After six weeks she would grieve another last goodbye and take down the ironing board. And maybe, just maybe today, would be the day she would put clean sheets on the bed.

Thank you, Holy God, for permanent-press shirts, the variety of chores we enjoy, knowing what pleases us, and our senses that trigger memories. We also thank you for rituals that enrich our lives, the morning sun to lift our spirits, cards and letters from those who love us, and the courage to make it through another day. Amen.

Month by Month

There is a file in the drawer to the left of my desk labeled "Month to Month." I have had that file in my desk for most of my working years. Since I am a keeper of calendars, I very religiously have tucked those pages in the file at the end of each month. I usually keep last year's pages in the back and add the new month in the front. I am always surprised by how many times I go to that file to check for a date or an appointment or when we visited someone.

I thought at first that I would call this book "Month by Month." *Of Seasons and Sparrows* was a more general choreography of how a year passes but this book gets down to the specifics. I have this attention to turning the pages of calendars in my DNA. My mother was heavily influenced by the passing of the months and had such a clear sense of monthly fashion that she always gave me plenty of warning to have her white slacks and her white "summer" purse and shoes at the nursing home before Memorial Day and all packed up for me to take home the day after Labor Day. On our kitchen table, as we were growing up, there was usually an appropriate decoration for the holiday of the month. The decorations were tiny, we had a very small kitchen table but there would be a small Easter basket or a shamrock or a pumpkin, often beside a little vase of flowers, especially pansies which were mom's favorites. There would be a turkey with a pleated tail, a small flag for the 4th of July, and of course Christmas decorations. Our favorite was a little mirror with "snow" around the edge for a skating rink. The snow was Ivory Flakes, our laundry soap. I don't remember any skaters but there was a tiny white sleigh with an old Santa that my sister and I both loved. The Santa's suit was well worn red velvet, soft to the touch.

As our children were growing, I tried to carry on the tradition, but to be honest, I remember months that just got away from me. But mostly, my sister and I continue to be calendar girls. I was reminded of that once again as I separated the Christmas red and green M&Ms into a red bowl for Valentines Day and a green bowl for St Patrick's Day. Perhaps everyone doesn't do this?

So it is that I have been reflecting on the months of the year, the color of months, the smell and sounds of them, and of course the taste of them. I hope my readers will enjoy the recipes I have included, along with the story of the recipe or the person I stole it from.

I am also aware that some of you will read the January and February stories while sitting by your pool so you'll just have to excuse my going on and on about snow and below zero weather. We Wisconsin folks love to talk about our terrible winter weather.

For any of you (OK for the two or three of you out there) who buy this book in November or March, you may want to start with the correct month when you start reading — just to keep things chronological. You will know who you are.

Thank you, Holy God, for good memories of the past, the passing of the months, the beauty of each season, and the rhythm of rituals that sustain us. Amen.

APRIL

The lime green of spring
Yellow goldfinches, daffodils, and rubber boots
April is my birthday month when
Rain can come as anything
Sleet or snow but we want to call it rain
Taxes are due and it is often the Easter month
The earth is back

The Prodigal Son — Luke 15:11-24

Then Jesus said, "There was a man who had two sons. The younger of them said to his father, 'Father, give me the share of the property that will belong to me.' So he divided his property between them. A few days later the younger son gathered all he had and traveled to a distant country, and there he squandered his property in dissolute living. When he had spent everything, a severe famine took place throughout that country, and he began to be in need. So he went and hired himself out to one of the citizens of that country, who sent him to his fields to feed the pigs. He would gladly have filled himself with the pods that the pigs were eating; and no one gave him anything. But when he came to himself he said, 'How many of my father's hired hands have bread enough and to spare, but here I am dying of hunger! I will get up and go to my father, and I will say to him, "Father, I have sinned against heaven and before you; I am no longer worthy to be called your son; treat me like one of your hired hands."' So he set off and went to his father. But while he was still far off, his father saw him and was filled with compassion; he ran and put his arms around him and kissed him. Then the son said to him, 'Father, I have sinned against heaven and before you; I am no longer worthy to be called your son.' But the father said to his slaves, 'Quickly, bring out a robe — the best one — and put it on him; put a ring on his finger and sandals on his feet. And get the fatted calf and kill it, and let us eat and celebrate; for this son of mine was dead and is alive again; he was lost and is found!' And they began to celebrate."

Since this is my birthday month, I thought I should write a bit about retirement. This is the first book I have written since I retired. But I do remember how I felt when I was working long hours and retirement seemed completely out of reach, so —

- I write with humility because I know there are those who will read these words who may never know the luxury of retiring.
- I write remembering there are those who will read these words who are still working and for whom retirement is a long way off.
- I write with a grateful heart because I know there are those who will read these words who may find retirement to be lonely and awkward.

For Aden and me it is a busy, splendid time. We didn't retire to not be busy — we retired to focus on other things. So it is that on a Thursday morning in March, I can be writing these words instead of being in a staff meeting or teaching a class. I pray that I may never take a moment of any of this for granted.

Thank you, Holy God, for retirement and the time to do new things, April showers, fathers and mothers who welcome us home, and new beginnings. Amen.

The Prissy Old Couch

For those of you who have read *Heading Home*, you may remember my story of the couch that we set out in the alley to get rid of. There is another couch in my life, a couch with an even longer history in our family than the alley couch. When we moved to Bethlehem, Pennsylvania in the 60s so my husband could attend seminary, we were assigned an apartment on the third floor of the old city library and the place came with furniture. Someone had cleaned out after an estate sale and brought usable pieces for students who arrived without furniture. We were very grateful. Thus began our relationship with the couch. She was an elegant old thing, even then, having seen better days when her upholstery had been bright and new. Now it was a kind of gray and you could no longer distinguish the original pattern. But it was sturdy and it was a place to sit — it had elegant bones, and a graceful, curving back. Aden went to work taking off the old nearly black layers of varnish and got down to the wood again. We discovered the couch was magically made. The back and the seat and the two end pieces popped out easily and I could wrap a length of fabric around each piece and we had a new, if slightly uncomfortable, couch.

At the end of our stay, no one else seemed to need a couch, so we moved it to our first parsonage where it sat proudly in front of the picture window. It was our one and only couch for at least the first three parsonages. Every few years, I would slap on another length of fabric and it would be good for another few years. By the late 90s, the couch was losing stuffing badly and before one of our moves, we dismantled the whole thing, including all the horsehair stuffing. Springs dangled dangerously and we hung the pieces of couch in our garage until we could decide what to do with it. Disposing of it didn't seem to be part of the plan. There was a hue and cry from the children. And to be honest, it wasn't easy to consider getting rid of a piece of furniture that we had been sitting on for 30 years. But after our move to Madison, it was reluctantly placed in the family garage sale. No one showed any interest in it, so a beloved family member took it home for her own. At great expense, the couch was reconditioned with new stuffing and new beautiful red upholstery with two matching green pillows. She was beautiful, though still rather uncomfortable. She took her place proudly in a newly redecorated living room of sister, Roberta. It was still in the family.

A couple of years later, sister Roberta moved to a new house and there wasn't the perfect place for the couch. The call came. Didn't we want the couch back? Didn't we want to keep it in the family? I guess we did!

So now she sits in our log cabin next to the wood stove and the boxes of kindling and stacks of wood for the fire. She has her back to a log wall, in front of big windows looking out into the woods and she looks quite fine, though a little out of place. She looks like our prissy old aunt, smelling of lavender and wearing lace at her throat, coming for tea. We love her still.

Thank you, Holy God, for things that last, stories that our furniture can tell, family members that see value, and for the restoration of things and people. Amen.

Aging Gracelessly

*I*t all began when I went to the doctor for my "Medicare" physical. He is very young and even though it is a cliché, I do have clothes older than my wonderful doctor. But actually I was feeling pretty spry. I had been eating well, had lost a few pounds, and had been exercising regularly. My physical began routinely. Weight? — good. Any new medications? I'm always interested in this. I envision myself at the pharmacy — "I'll take a couple of months of that new stuff I've seen advertised in all the magazines." Wouldn't my doctor be the first to know if I was taking any new medications? Perhaps some other doctor had prescribed something? No — no new medications. Check the ears, nose, and throat. Check the reflexes. Any pain? No. Back to the charts. Then my dear doctor began the old age conversation. "At your age, I want you to start having flu shots every year. And at your age, I'd like you to have a pneumonia shot. And at your age, you should probably consider having the shingles vaccine. And there are several tests that we won't continue now that you are 65."

When I came into the doctor's office, I felt fine but in 15 minutes, I was beginning to feel a bit puny. I had changed from a rather spry woman to a 65 year-old. Maybe I did have a little pain. What about this thing growing on my scalp? Should I have that taken off? I felt like I had stepped into the portrait of Dorian Gray, and any minute my hair would turn white and long whiskers would grow out of my chin.

Certain other things have been happening lately. I went into my local bath and soap place and asked for my favorite liquid soap that I had been using for over 10 years. The young salesclerk said, "Oh, we don't carry that anymore." I expressed my disappointment and she said, "Sometimes we order that for our big sale in December and July. That item is now considered a 'classic' so we don't carry it in the store anymore." Since when did my favorite soap become a classic? I went to buy my favorite breakfast cereal. "What happened to that?" I asked the manager of my local grocery store and he said, "Oh, we haven't carried that for a long time."

The place where I usually get my 35mm film developed has closed. And I am not sure which side of the digital divide I should be on. Things are going way too fast.

I have always been glad to be the age I am but I find myself changing too. I notice that I have started calling folks, "dears." Maybe it's because I'm 65. At my age, maybe this is supposed to happen.

After her recent birthday I asked my granddaughter, Maddie, how she felt now that she was four years-old. She said, "I am not four — I am turning into five. Grandma, what are you turning into?" I replied, "I am turning into an old lady, my dear."

Thank you, Holy God, for birthdays to mark our years, for doctors who ask the right questions, the willingness to be open to change, and for grandchildren who keep us young. Amen.

Navy Blue Capes

In the early 70s, I was a young mother, with two toddlers, living in the same small town that I have returned to in retirement. Friends who were also young mothers made life fun and interesting and full. During a program held at our church, a missionary doctor presented an opportunity for a hands-on mission project, and my friend and I volunteered immediately. It was something we could do, and a four-year adventure began.

Our Moravian hospital in Nicaragua had a very successful nurses' training school and a dream of these young nurses was to have a cape to mark their graduation. Our task was to sew navy blue capes with a bright red lining. Each year, we received the names and the heights of the graduates and we set to work. With four young children, there were times when the sewing got a little hectic, but Nancy and I enjoyed many happy hours preparing the capes and then worrying whether they would get to Nicaragua in time for the big day. Eventually, the war in Nicaragua disrupted the nursing program and Nancy and I went on to other things.

In 1995, at a women's retreat in the mountains of southern California, women huddled around a huge fireplace. We began to get acquainted with one another. Around the circle we went, giving our names, where we were from, what we had done as careers, the usual introduction fare. One of the women said she had trained as a nurse in Nicaragua before the war and then had moved with most of her family to California. I said casually, that I had sewn some capes for nurses back in the 70s. Looking a bit confused at first, Hilda replied, "I think I received one of those capes in 1973."

We spent a lovely few minutes sharing the wonderful story of her graduation day and the excitement of receiving the capes, including the pictures they took with one edge of the cape thrown back over the shoulder to reveal the beautiful red lining.

In 2005, at another women's retreat in San Clemente, California, as we gathered for our first session, one of the women approached me. In her hands was a plastic bag and inside was the navy blue cape she had worn in 1973. Accompanying the cape was a picture of Hilda on her graduation day, with flowers pinned to one edge of the cape, thrown back over her shoulder to reveal the red lining. We spent a few more lovely minutes, this time sharing how the cape had been left in Nicaragua, then rescued by a family member, and finally returned to Hilda.

Mission is about people and Nancy and I never dreamed all those years ago that we would meet one of the receivers of our small mission project. And Hilda never dreamed that she would meet one of the young mothers who had sent the capes. Most of us never see the fruits of our labors and that is probably the way it should be, but once in awhile, we are connected, over the years, over the miles, and that connection warms our hearts and makes us smile. And perhaps it makes us able to say "yes" again when the opportunity comes. Nancy and I are glad we said "yes" so many years ago. We have been blessed.

Thank you, Holy God, for trained nurses in blue capes, the reminder that mission is about people, opportunities to serve, and the willingness and courage to say yes. Amen.

May

The month of lace and lavender
Pastels and patent leather shoes
Miniature flowers in our woods
In shades of pink and white
May is for mothers and maidens
And fine ladies going to tea
We wait for that first really warm day when
The air is soft and we can go without a coat

Our biblical short story speaks of women, caring for others, seeking knowledge — always the tug is there for women to be two places at the same time.

Jesus Visits Martha and Mary — Luke 10:38-42

Now as they went on their way, he entered a certain village, where a woman named Martha welcomed him into her home. She had a sister named Mary, who sat at the Lord's feet and listened to what he was saying. But Martha was distracted by her many tasks; so she came to him and asked, "Lord, do you not care that my sister has left me to do all the work by myself? Tell her then to help me." But the Lord answered her, "Martha, Martha, you are worried and distracted by many things; there is need of only one thing. Mary has chosen the better part, which will not be taken away from her."

May is also the month of the first rite of summer, Memorial Day. So it's time to dust off the picnic table, find the paper plates, and get ready for the first official cook-out. This recipe is a sure-fire hit. It was given to me by a fellow teacher in my first years of teaching sixth grade. The recipe card is a smeary mess of sauce ingredients.

The recipe works well on the grill but you will have to use your own method for testing to see when the chicken is done. I don't grill. I usually bake it in a 350 degree oven in the cool part of the day and then warm it up before eating. It's good cold, too.

Chicken Baked with Honey Sauce

¼ cup honey
3 tablespoons soy sauce
2 tablespoons ketchup
¼ teaspoon ginger
½ cup chicken broth (or you can just use water)

Simmer the 5 ingredients for 8 minutes. When cool, pour sauce over enough chicken for 4 people and marinate at least an hour. I often marinate it overnight in the refrigerator. Bake uncovered in sauce 1 ½ – 2 hours in a 350 degree oven.

Thank you, Holy God, for tea parties, spring days that renew us, lives of study and service, and lives of caregiving and achievement. Amen.

Fierce Mothers

This summer has been a time to think about mothers. My own mother is slowly dying and this week I am reveling in having my daughters visit me. I love the experience of seeing my daughters in their roles as mothers. Between them, they are mothers to my spectacular three little granddaughters. And my greatest joy is to watch our girls watch their girls. I am proud to say they are fierce mothers. Though different in their parenting approach, they both are vigilant in their care.

What a blessing that is — to be raised by mothers who worry about your well-being. And the saddest thing in the world must be the dull, unfeeling eyes of mothers, unable to respond to the cries of their children. Maybe they are tired or ill. Maybe they are being hurt themselves. Maybe they do not know they have the capacity to care. Maybe they have given up.

One afternoon I experienced a mom and her children in the grocery store. She was clearly overwhelmed, with a baby in the cart and a toddler who she held tightly by the hand. But she has too many children to care for because a third child shuffled along behind. He looked miserable. His chin quivered and tears streamed down his cheek. When he did let out a whimper, the mother said, "I don't want to hear another sound out of you." So there was no more sound, just the tears and the trembling of tiny shoulders.

Now there are a million explanations for this scene. This oldest child might have done something terrible. He might have had a temper tantrum because he wanted her to buy him something. He might have been tired. Surely she was tired. And we can imagine the things that would have made this mother reply in that way. There certainly were times with three small children that I said things like that. But my heart nearly broke just to see the misery of that small child. I would hope for all small children to have mothers and fathers who would fiercely care for them. I would hope for parents who would look for dangers to keep them safe — anticipate things that would frighten or harm — search for the best foods and schools and experiences for their child.

These are the thoughts that go through my mind as I watch my girls. My oldest holds her young daughter who has just bumped her head. My youngest patiently brings new things for her toddler to play with, to keep her out of the things at Grandma's house that could harm. And the theme of motherhood is repeated everywhere we look, mother birds feeding their babies, an old mama bear watching out for her young cub, and a turkey mother strutting down the path corralling her fuzzy babies as she goes.

Every day is Mother's Day! And I am grateful for the gifts and graces our girls demonstrate as they are mothers. Of course, they would be creative, funny, practical, and nurturing — they are my daughters — they had me as a mother!

Thank you, Holy God, for all mothers — animal and human, the patience of mothers and fathers who parent well, times spent with family, and the wisdom of adults to guide their young. Amen.

Random Thoughts from a Random Mother

Twenty-five years ago I wrote a very long epistle to some friends who were having their first child. I was up to my hips in children at the time and starting seminary. The pages of advice surfaced on an old disk and I smiled as I read some of the old-fashioned ideas, but there are some things I feel still ring true.

Random Thoughts from a Random Mother

This paper requires a bit of explanation if it is to be of any help to you. First of all, you have a right to expect that I am qualified to speak on such a subject. My qualifications are these:

1. There are three squirmy beings in the basement watching cartoons, which will testify to the fact that I have fulfilled the required hours as mother.

2. There is a guinea pig in the basement that seems to be sick; there is a very wet cocker spaniel sleeping on my bed; and there is a month old kitten in the upstairs bathroom that will only eat out of my cereal bowl — all of which point clearly to the fact that I am indeed random.

Being a very structured person, it pains me to inform you that living with children will be exactly like the outline of this paper — playing it by ear, by the seat of your pants, winging it as it were. But here goes:

Try never to say, "Hosea doesn't eat green beans," because then Hosea never will. Better to explain to your critics that Hosea just isn't in the mood for green beans today but you're sure he will be tomorrow.

Being happy is a child's responsibility and play is their job.

There will be times when it is absolutely essential and necessary that Erma and Hosea are a priority, like when they are sick or going through an emotional crisis.

And there will also be times when your marriage will be the priority. Remember that babies are a fleeting moment in your life. They need to see you together, as a unit. They need to see you work as a team. The child needs both of you. They need to hear you say that you love one another.

My wish for you is that living with your baby will be as much fun as living with ours has been. And it only gets better. That's my parting remark. Don't let people make you miss each good day. People have a way of wishing away each phase your baby is in with ominous warnings of "wait till they start talking." Or walking, or getting into things, or driving, or... babies do things in phases. And just when you think you can't stand one more minute of their throwing their spoon at you every morning, they will stop and do something else. But every phase is good. Just enjoy each day and what your baby can do in that day. It won't be long before you two will be writing your own book of baby advice. Babies make experts of us all!

Thank you, Holy God, for babies and toddlers, marriages that thrive, knowing when to hold on to our children and when to let go, and the wisdom from those who have gone before us. Amen.

Oxygen Mask First

Remove the safety card from the seat pocket in front of you and follow along. Keep your seat belt tightened, low and tight across your lap. There are four exit doors marked overhead with an exit sign. Your nearest exit may be behind you. If needed, an oxygen mask will automatically drop from the overhead panel. If traveling with small children, make sure you put on your face mask before helping your child. Pull the mask firmly toward you to start the oxygen flowing. Oxygen will be flowing, although the bag will not inflate.

I have heard this safety announcement, probably a hundred times and I'm always struck with the exact words that are used in spite of the airline. They all must have the same manual. Once I caught a rookie flight attendant sitting on the jump seat reading the instructions from a small piece of hand-written paper. I'm not sure why I was walking to the front of the plane while she was doing this but I'm sure that I was reprimanded and she didn't have to read that off her hand-written paper.

Another time, a seasoned flight attendant went barreling through her instructions but tucked this into the oxygen speech — "if you are sitting next to a child or someone who is acting like a child…" Only a couple of us caught the joke.

Once I was on a plane filled with teenagers going to Europe, probably for a summer abroad. The whole front of the plane was nothing but teenagers. When the attendant started her spiel, they pantomimed the presentation. With drill team precision, they lifted their hands to show the seat belt being safely buckled, pointed out the lights in the aisle and the exit doors front and back and the oxygen compartments overhead.

Make sure you put your oxygen mask on first before helping others. Those of us who were taught as children not to be selfish have a hard time with this concept. We may know it in our head but taking care of ourselves first just seems alien, even though we may know it's the thing to do. We are so wary of that slippery slope, when we step over the line when things become all about us. That line is what we worry about. But now and then we need to be reminded — you have to take care of yourself first, then you can serve others.

And how do you do that? Many years ago, I heard this maxim for taking care of yourself, of staying healthy and full of energy for a life of faith and service:

- Detach daily — let your mind go on vacation for at least an hour a day — walk, meditate, breathe
- Withdraw weekly — it's called a day off — it's called a Sabbath — take it
- Migrate monthly — get out of town for two or three days
- Abandon annually — get out of the country (or at least pretty far away)

And always remember to put on your oxygen mask first.

Thank you, Holy God, for people who help us stay healthy, days off and yearly vacations, Sabbath and the wisdom to use it, and fresh air when we need a second wind. Amen.

June

And what is so rare as a day in June
This month is full of hope
Of harvest as gardens are planted
Of leisure as vacations are planned
The kind of month that children draw in crayon
Blue sky, green grass, and
White puffy clouds
Schools out — everyone gets crazy
There might be a day to get a little lazy

The Parable of the Sower — Mark 4:1-9

Again he began to teach beside the lake. Such a very large crowd gathered around him that he got into a boat on the lake and sat there, while the whole crowd was beside the lake on the land. He began to teach them many things in parables, and in his teaching he said to them: "Listen! A sower went out to sow. As he sowed, some seed fell on the path, and the birds came and ate it up. Other seed fell on rocky ground, where it did not have much soil, and it sprang up quickly, since it had no depth of soil. And when the sun rose, it was scorched; and since it had no root, it withered away. Other seed fell among thorns, and the thorns grew up and choked it, and it yielded no grain. Other seed fell into good soil and brought forth grain, growing up and increasing and yielding thirty and sixty and a hundredfold." And he said, "Let anyone with ears to hear listen!"

Everybody gets a little lazy and there might be time for a leisurely breakfast of "eggs in a bag." This recipe provides entertainment as well as a healthy way to start the day. This recipe, and several others in this book, is a gift from friend Nancy. She and I have been cooking up things together for decades.

Eggs in a Bag

Have guests write their name on a quart-sized freezer bag with permanent marker. Crack two eggs (large or extra-large) into the bag and shake to combine them.

Put out a variety of ingredients such as: cheeses, ham, onion, green pepper, tomato, hash browns, salsa, mushrooms, bacon bits, and avocado, etc. (I use dried minced onion, because the raw onion doesn't cook very well.)

Each guest adds the prepared ingredients of their choice to their bag and shakes it well. Make sure to get the air out of the bag and zip it up.

Place the bags into rolling, boiling water for exactly 13 minutes. You can cook 5-6 omelets in a large pot.

Be careful when you put the bags in the water — don't let the plastic get on the side of the pan, or it will melt! The bags need to float in the boiling water. Turn them over a couple of times so the eggs are cooked evenly. Open the bags and the omelet will roll out easily. Enjoy!

Thank you, Holy God, for sowers of seed and sowers of the Word, good earth to grow in, hours of leisure and days of fun, and family and friends who come for breakfast. Amen.

Irene Waters the Plant

I am not a plant person. Over the years, people have tried to inspire me to grow things but I've been pretty resistant about committing myself to keeping something green and alive — with one exception. Sometime during our ministry in California, someone gave us a jade plant. I neglected it in my usual way, forgetting to water it for long periods of time, and just leaving it alone as it sat on our patio in the sunny California climate. But it refused to die. When we moved to Pennsylvania in the early 90s, we brought the plant with us. It merrily continued to grow new leaves and every once in awhile, it shot out a pod-looking thing. I ignored it as much as possible but still it thrived. I repotted it several times because some green-thumbed person would instruct me to do so. In 2004 we moved to the woods and the plant got plunked down in front of the sunny window in our family room. When summer arrived, it went out on our sunny morning porch. Once outside I could hardly keep up — it sent out huge, dark, green shiny new leaves and by the time I brought it in for the winter, it was in another bigger new pot.

By last fall, the jade plant had become a serious, living thing. It really didn't fit in front of the window anymore and I could no longer lift it. Something had to be done so I surveyed my plant loving relatives, all of whom said I should trim it back but they weren't sure how. So I trimmed it as mercifully as I could and I even took some slips in case it could take root and I could start over. Alas, the plant died. And I experienced freedom and relief. No more trying to figure out how to care for it when we were away for long periods of time. No more lugging it back and forth to the porch.

Some of us are not good with plants but some of us are, people like Irene. I met Irene at a conference. Six hundred worshipped together in a large chapel that was very hot. In the middle of a hymn Irene bolted from her seat in the back of the church. She rushed to the front and grabbed a potted plant that sat there. The potted plant sat drooping badly in the heat. As she passed my pew, she said, "I can't stand it anymore." Off she marched carrying the drooping plant in front of her like a wriggling toddler needing a bath. In a few minutes, she returned with the plant. It looked exactly the same to me. Its leaves still drooped over the sides of the pot. She set it down with purpose and returned to her seat.

As the service continued, I watched the plant. For several minutes, nothing happened and 'oh, me of little faith,' I thought "too little, too late." But then, little by little, imperceptibly, that thirsty plant, the drooping, nearly dead plant, began to come to life.

It didn't matter what was happening in the rest of the service. I was watching the plant. A couple of leaves began to rise and even though I was watching as closely as I could, I couldn't really see the moment when the stalks began to gain strength and stand up. But at some point, there it was — a beautiful, glossy leafed plant. Someone told me it was a Peace Lily. It really was a beautiful plant — maybe I should buy one!

Thank you, Holy God, for people who can grow plants, green plants that replenish the air, water that sustains us, and for people who lift us up. Amen.

The 18-Wheeler

Many years ago, I had a weekly commute to visit my stepmother who was ill. I traveled the six hours by car and on one of those trips, I was joined by a friend. We left very early in the morning and were talking a mile a minute. I was driving, sticking to the interstate highways to make good time. We talked and laughed and the miles flew by. Things were going swimmingly, until ahead of me I saw a stoplight. I said, "I don't think we are on the interstate anymore." And we both convulsed into laughter. No problem — we would stop for breakfast and figure out where we went wrong.

We pulled into a diner. The parking lot was full of trucks. It was a long narrow diner — just enough room for the counter and a row of stools. Three were empty, every other one occupied by a trucker, a big husky man who perched on the spindly seat. We sat down, ordered our breakfast, and tried to get control of the laughter that kept bubbling up. Where did that interstate highway go? We didn't remember an exit ramp but oh well, we were here now and breakfast would taste good.

As we were eating our eggs and toast, the man next to me leaned over and quietly asked, "You girls driving an 18-wheeler?" I said, "Not exactly." I told him that apparently we had made a wrong turn and we needed help in getting back to the highway.

What happened then was part drama, part dance, mostly community. All the truckers up and down the counter felt it was their duty to get us back on the road. And they acted it out.

OK — here is where we are now. They set down the napkin holder. You take a left at the stoplight. Knives and spoons lined up to make a path. Three blocks and on the right, you'll see a church. The ketchup bottle made a lovely church with its white capped steeple. After you get by the church, you go another half block and you'll see the entrance ramp to the highway. Most of the truckers agreed this was the best way but one trucker got off his stool and rearranged several of the knives and spoons to indicate a shortcut to the Church of the First Ketchup.

As we were finishing our breakfast, another customer arrived to take the empty stool. He was precisely dressed — button-down oxford shirt, blue tie, khaki slacks. The waitress arrived with her order pad and a stubby pencil. He began to give her his order. "I would like two eggs over easy. I like the whites set but the yolk still runny. With that I would like three strips of bacon, very crisp, whole wheat toast — no butter. And hash browns — no onions and light on the salt and pepper and cooked until tender but not crispy." By this time, he had all of our attention. The waitress stood in front of him, holding her order pad at shoulder height. When he had finished, she said absolutely nothing for several seconds. Then she very slowly turned to the window where the cook waited. "Number two," she said. That's all — just the number two and my friend and I managed to pay the bill and get outside before we once more burst into laughter.

Thank you, Holy God, for friends to laugh with, moments of expressed community, the great variety of people we meet, and folks who simply call it like it is. Amen.

Things My Mother Said

I am in the process of transcribing my diaries. I began writing four lines each night in 1956. I have continued to this very day. My intent in this project is to transcribe those four lines (or most of them) into a word document, making comments and asking questions along the way — a kind of annotated version of my life.

What makes me smile is that as a 14 year-old writer I was so taken with clichés. These are some that I found.

- back to the old grind
- I'm really in my glory now
- the flame is still flickering
- I'm bushed

I think it was in my DNA. My mother loved words too — she had a saying for almost every event and way up into her 90s she was still doing crossword puzzles, in ink!

Here are some of the things my mother said:

- We're off like a herd of turtles.
- You can't eat meat without bread or potatoes.
- There is no rest for the wicked.
- Off we go like a dirty shirt.
- You can't get blood out of a turnip.

And here are some more classic quotes from my mom — We were having mom's hearing aids checked and without them, mom couldn't hear a thing. Since there was all that silence, she chattered on and on to me but mostly to the technician who was ignoring the conversation entirely. She never looked in mom's direction, staying focused on the tiny intricate wire and plastic of the hearing aid. Finally, in exasperation, my mom said, directly to the technician, "My daughter is a bishop. She's not just anybody, you know." The technician caved. Mom had finally got her attention.

For Christmas, I was so pleased to have found a new book by a favorite author of hers. About a week later, she called. "I am so disgusted," she said. "Oh, I'm sorry," I said. "Didn't you like the book?" "I loved it," she said, "but it didn't finish. She's going to write the sequel but it won't be coming out till next September. I might be dead by then and I'll never know how it turned out!" As it turned out, that is exactly what happened.

Mom loved it when my sister and I sang "How Great Thou Art" for her and had requested that we sing it at her memorial service. So shortly after her hospitalization in March, I took my uke along and we did a little singing. Mom chatted a bit and then shut her eyes. We launched into a quiet version of "How Great Thou Art." When we had finished, mom opened her eyes and said, "I had better not die for a long time because you girls still have a little work to do on that."

After mom's 94th birthday, she and I were playing cards. She was concerned about some medication she was taking and she hadn't felt like going down to breakfast. She smiled and said, "Well, I guess I just have to get used to the idea that I can't do everything that I could do when I was 93!"

Thank you, Holy God, for the ritual of words, a sense of humor, the gifts of each passing age, and the quiet confidence and wisdom of old age. Amen.

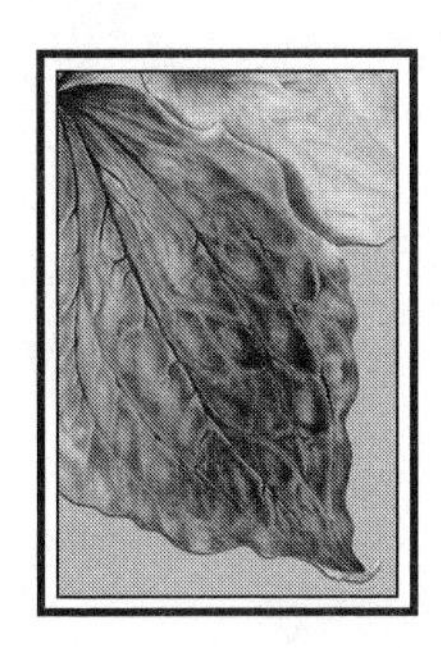

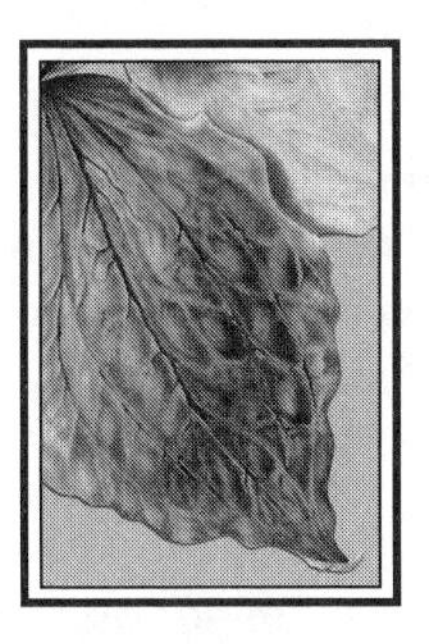

Writing In Spurts

When I retired, I imagined myself getting up every morning, grabbing a cup of coffee and going to my chair in the loft and writing. I would be as disciplined as all the great writers. I would write three pages a day, every day. But at first, I told myself, I needed to get settled. And then I told myself I needed to get into a new routine. Months went by. I finally told myself that I am a person who writes in spurts.

I am writing this at a water park in Wisconsin in January. It's 5 degrees outside and about 80 degrees in here; 80 degrees and moist and smelling of chlorine. I threw a notebook in with my swimming suit and here I sit guarding the family's valuables while they are swimming and riding rafts and being very wet.

Occasionally, a wet person goes by the table and drips water on my notebook. And occasionally, my granddaughter, Cecilia, crawls into my lap with a cold little wet body and I'm wet all over. But for some inexplicable reason, I can't stop writing.

It's always this way. I write on napkins in restaurants. I write on the back of my ticket folder on airplanes. I write in the car on the back of receipts. I write during the prelude on the back of my bulletin and I try very hard never to write during the sermon. But it's very hard. I write in the middle of the night, in the dark on a little notepad that my friend gave me many years ago. When I pull the pen out, a little light goes on and I can see to write a little.

Writing is never what I expect it to be. I have prepared a very special writing area for myself. I have a box of pencils, many notebooks, a pile of writing books for inspiration, a small table for my coffee cup, and a comfy shawl for my shoulders. I have never written there. I do other things there but I don't write. I like to think of myself as a person who is disciplined and careful. But writing for me is a surprisingly messy business.

And I write for very different reasons. I write when something happens to me that is so funny or so sad or so scary that I feel compelled to put it on paper. Sometimes it comes out as an essay because I am an essayist (see *First Things First*). Sometimes it comes out as a poem and sometimes it comes out as a short story that Frances likes to tell in her own words. In that case, it helps me to have some distance from the intense feelings.

I always write in pencil not only because I can easily erase but because I feel like I can go faster with a pencil. I use an "Eversharp" with .5 lead and when I am on a roll, the lead flies.

Of course, there are disadvantages to using pencils — my writing gets a little smeary at times and I struggle to read what I have written. It's especially hard to read when wet, which it is now, as granddaughter Nadia arrives for a hug. More later.

Thank you, Holy God, for time to think and read and write, moments in my life that I want to remember, words that come from secret places, and for people who might want to read what I write. Amen.

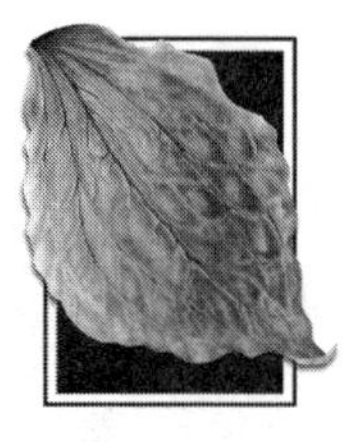

July

It's all about the red, white, and blue
With a splash of lemonade thrown in
Flags and red-checked tablecloths
The smell of suntan lotion
And lots of mosquito repellent
The month gets hot and we need water to drink with ice
Water to swim in and to sail on and to camp beside

Jesus Walks on Water — Matthew 14:22-33

Immediately he made the disciples get into the boat and go on ahead to the other side, while he dismissed the crowds. And after he had dismissed the crowds, he went up the mountain by himself to pray. When evening came, he was there alone, but by this time the boat, battered by the waves, was far from the land, for the wind was against them. And early in the morning he came walking towards them on the lake. But when the disciples saw him walking on the lake, they were terrified, saying, "It is a ghost!" And they cried out in fear. But immediately Jesus spoke to them and said, "Take heart, it is I; do not be afraid."

Peter answered him, "Lord, if it is you, command me to come to you on the water." He said, "Come." So Peter got out of the boat, started walking on the water, and came towards Jesus. But when he noticed the strong wind, he became frightened, and beginning to sink, he cried out, "Lord, save me!" Jesus immediately reached out his hand and caught him, saying to him, "You of little faith, why did you doubt?" When they got into the boat, the wind ceased. And those in the boat worshipped him, saying, "Truly you are the Son of God."

If we get tired of grilling out, we can cook up a batch of sloppy joe mix and serve a crowd. This recipe is from Clara who was the matriarch of the little church I grew up in. The recipe says "Clara's Sloppy Joe Recipe for 60 buns" but it doesn't make quite that much. I do believe our buns are bigger these days. At every event at Lakeview Moravian Church, we enjoyed sloppy joes, carrot and celery sticks, dill pickles, and potato chips. It doesn't get much better than that.

Clara's Sloppy Joe Recipe for 60 buns

5 pounds of hamburger — use more to make it meatier
2 cans tomato soup
2 bottles of chili sauce
1 large stalk of celery, chopped fine*
4 large onions, chopped
a little vinegar or lemon juice
½ cup brown sugar
salt and pepper

Brown meat and drain off grease. Add other ingredients and simmer until vegetables are cooked through. Or you can throw the whole thing in a crock pot and forget about it.

* I am never sure what a "stalk" of celery is but I put a whole bunch in because we like celery.

Thank you, Holy God, for memories of childhood that delight us, water that refreshes, being saved by someone when we are going down for the third time, and being saved by Christ all the time. Amen.

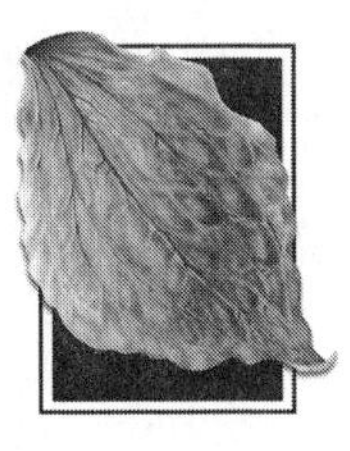

Mother Leaving Me

Today is my birthday and my mother didn't send me a card. She didn't send the card with the check folded in half inside, that check as regular as the sun, coming each year, at least two days before my actual birthday. That check has come every year since I left for college in 1960, always for the perfect amount of money for my birthday, determined by a formula that only my mother knew. That check has come with "Happy Birthday, Kay" written on that line in the bottom left hand corner.

Not getting a birthday card was not the first sign that my mother was leaving but it was the most poignant. Within a few days, my mother no longer answered the phone when I called. Those twice weekly phone calls had been a lifeline for both of us. I would call from my travels and she would try to remember or guess where I was calling from. Many days find me reaching for the phone to dial the familiar number.

She wasn't talking on the phone anymore but we still had our weekly visits. Though we couldn't go out for lunch, I would sit with her while she ate and then we would play cards. But soon the day came when she stared earnestly at her hand of Skip-Bo and didn't have the slightest idea of what to do with them. I told her I was pretty tired and maybe we should just enjoy the rest of our time together by sharing the news.

She couldn't play cards anymore but we could still enjoy talking. She loved telling me about the latest Bingo games and adventures with her friends. I shared funny stories from the granddaughters and great-granddaughters. But very soon, she stopped talking. She listened intently as I told stories and showed her pictures but about the only words that came out were labored. "Darling" she said as I showed her new pictures of baby Maddie, her youngest great-granddaughter. Soon our visits consisted of taking her for a ride around the facility, letting everyone hug her and tell her how much they missed her at meals and Bingo.

Then came the day when she no longer could be up in the chair but lay quietly, with the help of medication. I took to bringing "hand" work as she called it — embroidery or needlework of any kind. She dozed mostly but seemed to enjoy having me sit next to her bed while she rested. There was no conversation but once she looked over at me and said, "You need more light." It was as clear as anything she had ever said. Those were the last words she would say. And I believe those "mother" words, words that she had been saying to me since I was old enough to look at a book, came from a deep well of memory that was still intact in her dying body.

And then the day came — the day I had most dreaded, when she opened her eyes and looked at me as if I was some kind neighbor who had stopped by. She smiled slightly but then I knew, my mother had left me.

Thank you, Holy God, for birthday cards and letters, mothers who never stop being our mothers, and for generations which help us know who we are. Amen.

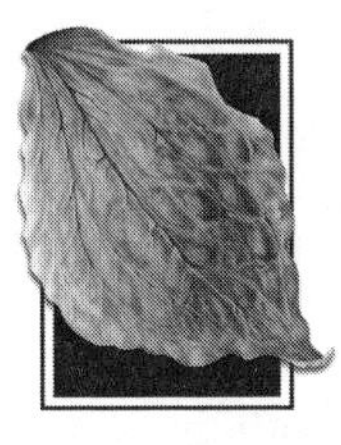

No More Tangles

When our daughter was little with a mass of dark, curly hair, we went through bottles of "No More Tangles." It made it a little easier to put a brush through her heavy head of hair. And I am still untangling things.

One of my favorite pastimes is untangling skeins of snarled and knotted yarn. I have spent many happy moments sitting quietly with a mess of yarn in my lap. I'm not normally a very patient person but I have almost infinite patience with a mess of yarn. Finding an end, rolling a bit of a ball, then threading it through one set of knots after another is very satisfying. It is probably like my friend who likes to iron out the wrinkles of her day. (See *Ironing.*) I like to tie up the loose ends of my life.

At our junior high camp a couple of years ago, I brought my laundry basket full of yarn with a bunch of needles for the kids to use to learn to knit. At the bottom of the basket was a pile of yarn — all different colors rolled into one big mess. I thought I would have time to sort it out when I wasn't working with the kids. That proved not to be the case, but the tangled yarn proved useful in another way.

The first day of camp, one of the first year campers was having a rough time. She didn't think she knew anybody and she was too shy to get acquainted. She wanted to go home. The camp director persuaded her to give it the afternoon and if she still wanted to leave, she would call her parents when they got home from work and they could come for her. In the meantime, the camp director led her over to the table where I was giving knitting lessons. We started out showing her how to knit but she was so nervous and anxious, there was no way she was going to be able to learn to knit. In desperation, I asked her if she would help me untangle the mess of yarn at the bottom of the laundry basket. I dumped the whole mess in her lap and showed her how to roll a ball with a loose end. I showed her how to look for other beginning places with loose ends to make other balls.

I turned my attention to the other campers as they tried to master the art of knit and purl. Every once in a while I would look over to my young homesick one. She was sitting contentedly, totally engrossed in her project. And slowly, a small pile of balls of yarn appeared on the table, each one painstakingly untangled from the larger mess. And slowly the untangler was being drawn in too. And campers shyly introduced themselves, as they struggled with their knitting projects. By the end of the afternoon, all the yarn was corralled in perfect little balls and a bevy of little girls with their new friend in tow, hurried off to supper.

It would be a grand thing if life were as easy to untangle. When I am at loose ends, I would love for someone to be able to find a beginning place in me and untangle things. But until then, I will continue to work with yarn and the things I can untangle. It will have to be enough.

Thank you, Holy God, for messes that can be untangled, patience to look for a place to start, all who serve our children in youth programs, and the ability to sometimes be able to tie up loose ends. Amen.

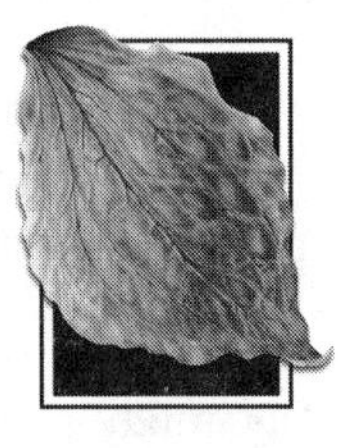

Untangling Yarn

I did a retreat for a congregation and one of the closing activities for the program on Saturday involved yarn. We grown-ups all sat on chairs in a circle, each holding a small ball of brightly colored yarn. We had been speaking about the church and about the connectedness we shared with one another. One by one they named the people with whom they were connected, through activities in the church, study groups, personal friendships, family connections, and mission projects. As each person spoke, they held on to the end of the yarn and then tossed the ball of yarn to someone else in the circle. They tossed it to someone with whom they had a connection, who was part of their story. As the sharing continued, the balls moved back and forth across the circle until a multi-colored web of yarn lay between us. Each person had a fistful of different colored yarn.

When the sharing was coming to an end, we stood in the circle and viewed our masterpiece, our bright web of connection. We saw this web as the support for our life of faith. I asked each person to lift the yarn web up so we could see its unique beauty.

As things happen, the children had been watching a video and at the precise moment we all had the web lifted, the children entered the room. No one said anything but immediately the children crawled under the grown-ups' legs into the circle. They laid down on the floor under the beautiful yarn web. There were the congregation's children safe under the protective web of the church. It was a beautiful moment. We ended with a prayer of thanksgiving. When the prayer had ended, we invited the children to scurry out and dropped the yarn web back to the floor. It was time to go to supper so I gathered up the yarn and threw it in a basket, intending to throw the whole thing away. Several minutes later, as people milled around, someone took the mess of yarn out of the basket. Several other folks joined her and started working on the yarn. They each took a different color and began to untangle the yarn. In and out, over and under, they worked, until once again the yarn was rolled up into little compact balls.

Life is complicated and there is much in our lives that isn't easy to untangle and get back into manageable compartments. Maybe that it is why it is so satisfying to untangle baskets full of brightly colored yarn.

Thank you, Holy God, for people who are led to attend retreats and conferences, the church's children, people who love a challenge, and the webs of relationship that connect us. Amen.

AUGUST

This month is sunflower yellow
With a rainbow of harvest colors
Eggplant purple and carrot orange
Green spinach and red tomatoes
But August goes too quickly
It races by with summer's last things
There is the foreshadowing of fall
Buying school clothes
And putting food up for the winter

The Woman at the Well — John 4:7-15

A Samaritan woman came to draw water, and Jesus said to her, "Give me a drink." (His disciples had gone to the city to buy food.) The Samaritan woman said to him, "How is it that you, a Jew, ask a drink of me, a woman of Samaria?" (Jews do not share things in common with Samaritans.) Jesus answered her, "If you knew the gift of God, and who it is that is saying to you, 'Give me a drink,' you would have asked him, and he would have given you living water." The woman said to him, "Sir, you have no bucket, and the well is deep. Where do you get that living water? Are you greater than our ancestor Jacob, who gave us the well, and with his sons and his flocks drank from it?" Jesus said to her, "Everyone who drinks of this water will be thirsty again, but those who drink of the water that I will give them will never be thirsty. The water that I will give will become in them a spring of water gushing up to eternal life." The woman said to him, "Sir, give me this water, so that I may never be thirsty or have to keep coming here to draw water."

Hot soup isn't a summer meal but I was thinking of all the beautiful broccoli that our farmer brings us. This is a very healthy Weight

Watchers recipe but don't tell anyone and they will love it. I call it Bisque because it sounds more elegant than soup.

Broccoli Bisque

Broccoli — the stems of three or four heads, cut into thin "coins"
(You can also use 1-2 large bags of frozen broccoli)
8 cups of chicken broth
minced onion to taste
8 ounces of 2% Velveeta Cheese, cut into cubes

Put the broth in a large pot and simmer the broccoli until it is very tender. There should be enough broth to cover the broccoli so you may have to add more broth.

Remove from stove and mash the broccoli, either with a submersible blender or a potato masher, until mashed well. Add the cheese and heat until smooth.

Thank you, Holy God, for vegetables warm from the sun, last days of summer, taste and smell, cool water in the heat of the day, and the refreshing, living water of Jesus Christ. Amen.

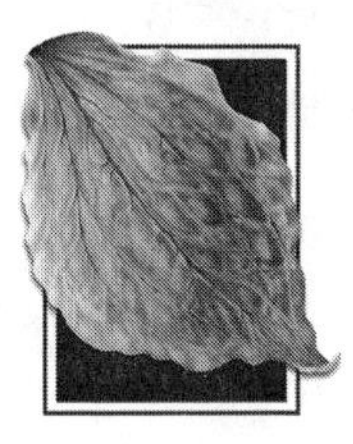

Same Name

There are some things that happen to a person that are just too quirky to share. When you say them out loud, they sound trivial and meaningless. They are moments like driving along listening to the radio and hearing an advertisement for a new apartment complex that is being built, then thinking about the location of the place, when all of a sudden my lights flashed on a huge sign and the entrance to the new apartment complex.

Another time, I was driving along, listening to public radio. At the top of the hour, a new segment came on: an interview with a meteorologist. And what had been a sunny afternoon suddenly turned into a tremendous thunderstorm, just as the weatherman described in detail the conditions needed to produce such a thunderstorm. These coincidences were so insignificant that I never bothered to tell anyone, but what happened to me last week was too unbelievable not to share.

I was flying into the Lehigh Valley in Pennsylvania, and I grabbed my suitcase and headed for the National Car Rental, where I had a car reserved for the weekend. I noticed a woman also headed in that direction from another flight, so I sped up a bit to get to the counter. Two young women stood behind the counter, waiting to help us. The agent spoke to the woman at my left and my agent asked me my name. I said, "Kay Ward." The agent at my left snapped her head up to look at me when I spoke. She said, "What did you say your name was?" I repeated my name. Then she turned to her customer and asked, "What is your name?" In my hearing now, she said, "My name is Kay Ward."

So there we were, two Kay Wards standing at a car rental counter, arriving at the same time, coming from different parts of the country, on different airplanes. The other Kay Ward and I had a good time getting acquainted — was this our real name? — maiden or married? — had this ever happened before? — while the rental agents tried to figure out the paperwork. The computers had produced two reservations with the name Kay Ward but with a mix of information and reservation data.

This was a story I couldn't wait to tell and I did, over and over. People smiled and told me about times that had happened to them. Some were shocked and many were speechless. Surely, there is a profound message in here somewhere.

I think you have to be wiser than I am to know what this means, if it means anything at all, but it might be about God's caring for us, counting even the hairs on our head. Or maybe it reminds us there is an order in the world when I so often experience it as chaos. Or maybe it reminds me that my little corner of the world is very small and the whole world is very big.

Whatever it means, and you probably have some ideas of your own, I know that it delighted me. I'm grateful my plane was late and I'm grateful to have shared this little human drama with a woman at the ABE airport, with that other Kay Ward.

Thank you, Holy God, for people we know by name, odd little happenings, surprises that delight us, and connections that help us know who we are. Amen.

Cell Phones

I'm on a delay at the airport. The minute the delay was announced, at least half the people sitting around me took out their cell phones and made a call. And most of them seem oblivious to those around us. What did we do before cell phones? Here are some snippets of the private calls I heard:

- I made it — I'm at the airport but there is a delay.
- Well, it depends on the buyer. I'll talk to her.
- Good morning — did I wake you up? Oh, I'm so sorry — we're on a delay.
- Look Jake — we'll give you $10,000 but you have to wear our jacket for the interview.
- They just pushed back the departure time another hour — we'll end up getting a hotel and staying in Chicago. Our sponsors will pay.
- I worked 70 hours overtime last month — so how is that working for me?
- I'm in Chicago and the sun is shining.
- Wouldn't you rather have it too big than too small?
- I hate to say this but I'm a friend of Fast Eddie's — yea — I'm usually running from him because he's always trying to sell me something. So I'm stuck with a 69 Mustang and an early 70s Chevelle. But I need titles for 'em and he suggested I give you a call.

A while ago, Aden and I had just settled ourselves in at a gate at O'Hare. Seated across from us was a young woman who was holding the crossword puzzle from the *USA Today*, which she had folded carefully, all set up to begin. Aden and I had finished reading the *USA Today* and I had completed the puzzle. We had already been there a long time.

The woman across from me began the puzzle and filled in a couple of words but soon hit a snag. In her left hand, she held her tiny cell phone and hit the speed dial. Without any greeting as the person answered the phone, she said, “What is a five letter word meaning grassy plant?” She went on to explain that the 3rd letter might be D but she wasn’t sure. I wanted to yell out SEDGE, but since everyone thinks they are having private conversations, I didn’t want to be rude. The young woman made many calls. I couldn’t tell if she was calling the same person each time but as our flight was called, she was working on “portly pres.”

There was something odd and wonderful at the same time about this encounter. Wonderful to be calling someone or many someones who seemed glad for the call and would be glad to help with the puzzle. But also odd that she needed to be in contact with someone far away, in the midst of a waiting area full of people. I couldn’t help but wonder how people had so much time to help her work on the puzzle — didn’t they have jobs?

No more musing. I have to call my husband on my cell phone. Excuse me!

Thank you, Holy God, for technology that connects us, the ability to travel safely, the circle of friends and family who surround us, and patience to get us home. Amen.

Leaving Your Children

It is time to go. The suitcases are packed and ready to be taken to the rental car. We stand making small talk, prolonging the exit. But they do have to go. Talk now turns to the next visit. How many months will it be? We'll talk on Saturday. Quick hugs and kisses and we hurriedly step out the door, dragging our stuff, hurrying because if we don't, we will all see the tears making our eyes all glistening and swimmy.

We're just back from taking our daughter, her husband, and our granddaughter to the airport to put them on a plane to fly home to California. Last week, we waved goodbye to our other daughter, husband, and two granddaughters to drive to Maryland. And I hate it! It breaks my heart to see them go.

I am absolutely certain that we are all exactly where we are supposed to be living and I wouldn't change a thing but it still is awful to say goodbye. It has never been an easy thing to do — dropping them off at kindergarten — taking them to camp — watching them leave the driveway with their new drivers license — leaving for college — all the leavings have broken my heart.

It's always the same. It always feels awful. There is in that moment of leaving, the urge to scream, "Come home with us — move next door — or we'll move there — we'll move next door to you!"

But we don't do that because our girls are happily married and have families of their own and have chosen to live places where we don't live. We don't do that because they are adults with lives of their own and because we have all chosen these different paths. But that doesn't make it any easier.

As bad as saying goodbye always is, one goodbye nearly killed me. Jenny, our oldest, was stationed in Namibia for her two-year commitment with the Peace Corps. We went to visit her halfway through her stint there and spent a wonderful two weeks traveling with her up north to her little village just a few miles from Angola. We loved seeing the country through her eyes and we spent three delicious days traveling through the Etoshe Game Park and then returned to Windhoek where we would return our rental car and catch a plane to Johannesburg. That meant that Jenny had to get back to her village, many hours away. We stayed overnight in Windhoek and then after breakfast drove Jenny out to the outskirts of town on the main highway going north. She would be hitchhiking back to Eenhana. She informed us that hitchhiking is an acceptable mode of transportation. It didn't seem very acceptable to me. She got out of the car and took her place along the road, with her backpack beside her. We got out, hugged her, got back in the car and I watched her get smaller and smaller in the rearview mirror. That was a goodbye I will never forget. The ride home for her was fine, good in fact, as she promised it would be. I cried all the way back to Windhoek.

Thank you, Holy God, for adult children who have their own lives, all safe travel, mercy when travel is dangerous, and for hearts that can be broken. Amen.

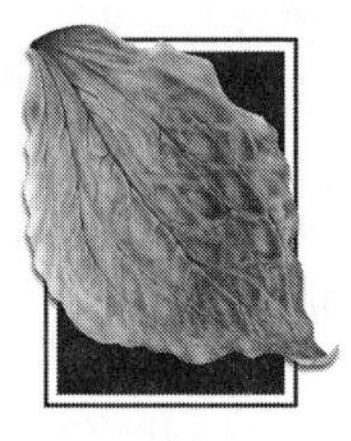

September

This month is school bus yellow
New boxes of crayons
Especially the 8 crayon box — the basics.
The last of the garden
Finds its way to kitchen counters
September offers a new beginning
Don't I need a new notebook?
Or a pencil box?

Jesus Heals a Crippled Woman — Luke 13:10-17

Now he was teaching in one of the synagogues on the sabbath. And just then there appeared a woman with a spirit that had crippled her for eighteen years. She was bent over and was quite unable to stand up straight. When Jesus saw her, he called her over and said, "Woman, you are set free from your ailment." When he laid his hands on her, immediately she stood up straight and began praising God. But the leader of the synagogue, indignant because Jesus had cured on the sabbath, kept saying to the crowd, "There are six days on which work ought to be done; come on those days and be cured, and not on the sabbath day." But the Lord answered him and said, "You hypocrites! Does not each of you on the sabbath untie his ox or his donkey from the manger, and lead it away to give it water? And ought not this woman, a daughter of Abraham whom Satan bound for eighteen long years, be set free from this bondage on the sabbath day?" When he said this, all his opponents were put to shame; and the entire crowd was rejoicing at all the wonderful things that he was doing.

In preparation for retirement, I read a book and then I shared it with my husband. It said that research had shown that no matter how folks planned for their retirement, whether to travel, take up a new hobby or volunteer, what most retirees spent most of their leisure time doing was watching television.

We really never discussed this but as we moved into our woods home, we just never bothered to get a TV hook-up. We had a DVD player and a VCR so we could watch movies when we wished, but we never did the cable or dish to receive programming.

Recently, we met some new folks and in passing mentioned that we hadn't watched such and such a program because we didn't have television. The man reached out to shake my hand and said, "I'm proud to know you." That struck me as curious — I don't know whether that says more about the man or about us. We are used to it now. And if truth be told, there are a few things we miss that we probably would enjoy, but they are so very few. We don't mean to be isolationists, pulling the woods in over our heads. We are faithful public radio listeners. And we are not crusaders about this. It's just at this time in our life, we are glad that we have made this decision. By the time I write another book, we might have changed our minds. Who knows?

Thank you, Holy God, for another new beginning in September, learning all our lives, leisure time with choices of what we do, and the relief when a weight is lifted from us. Amen.

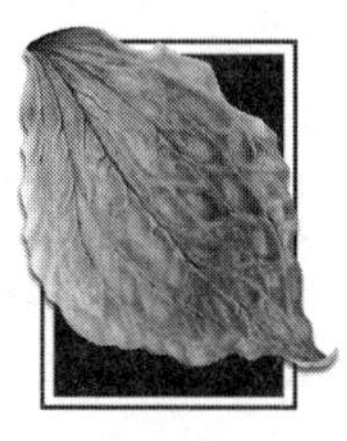

Precious Heirlooms

Every once in awhile I go on a tear to get rid of clutter in my life — to get rid of superfluous things. This usually begins in the closet. If I haven't worn it in a year, out it goes. The drive usually ends up in the dining room and the kitchen. I have an eclectic collection of dishes that I have hauled from one parsonage to the other all these years. Our china cupboard is especially loaded with dishes from others that I have clung to for years. As I stand there trying to decide which ones I could live without, a memory of my mom interrupts me.

It was the day we had taken mom from her nursing home back to her apartment to begin the sorting out of her things. It was clear by this time that she would never go back to her apartment. My sister and I had braced ourselves for a very sad day. We started in the kitchen. The new set of Corelle dishes held no special memories. The glasses and cups got divided up. Then we got to the upper shelves — there was the blue bowl. My sister and I both sighed. There were very few suppers I can ever remember that the blue bowl was not on the table. It held the canned vegetables at every supper. That was the only way we experienced vegetables in the cold winters of Wisconsin — DelMonte green beans or corn or LeSeur peas in the silver can. That blue bowl sometimes held cole slaw or canned fruit.

We solemnly carried the blue bowl into the living room, where Mom was going through pictures. We said, "Look, mom — the blue bowl." She took it in her bony hands and said, "You know, I never liked that bowl." What had been heart-rending moments before were transformed as my sister and I broke into laughter.

The story came back to me as I stood before my own china cupboard. I had new criteria now with which to judge. It was time for some serious pruning. I picked up a pottery bowl that I had been given decades before. I think I have used it once or twice in all those years but the truth was, I never really liked it. I didn't like the color or the shape and I have no idea who gave it to us. So I picked it up and put it in the bag for Goodwill. Just that one decision gave me the courage to pick up two fussy vases I had had since high school. I had hauled them, carefully wrapped in layers of paper for the last 50 years. They were Wedgwood blue with all sorts of fussy cherubs in white. Someone had told me they belonged to someone in the family but no one knew who. They were probably precious heirlooms but I have been more of a log cabin person than a Wedgwood, so with no regrets, I grabbed those vases and put them in the resale pile. I wished them well and hoped they would find a good home with a wonderful family who like Wedgwood blue vases with white cherubs. This, I've decided, is a gift of retirement — moving into a smaller home and having the time to assess one's belongings. I cling tightly to those things that tell a story or hold a memory. Other things? Out they go!

Thank you, Holy God, for the courage to get rid of things we don't need, log cabin people and Wedgwood Blue people, people who help us to reuse and recycle, and for the precious heirlooms of memories. Amen.

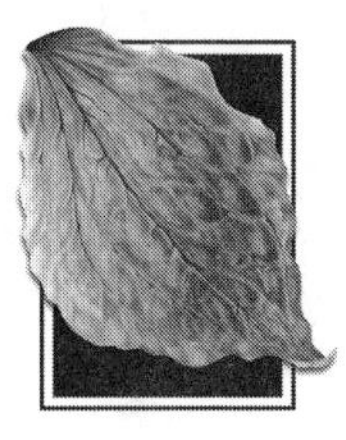

Women's Day and Family Circle

Aden brings in the mail and there they are — this month's issue of *Women's Day* and *Family Circle*. My association with the two grocery store magazines goes way back to my senior year of college. I was planning my wedding and dreaming of being the perfect housewife, so I began picking up the two magazines, *Women's Day* and *Family Circle*, in July of 1963. I am embarrassed to confess that I have found my way to the grocery story every month since then for the newest issues of those magazines. I have made the fancy cakes on the front cover. I have sewn clothes from the free patterns. I have crafted innumerable things we didn't need from the colorful pages of *Women's Day* or *Family Circle*. One of my more memorable Thanksgiving crafts was a cornucopia, which my sister and I made, requiring several boxes of aluminum foil and tubes of crescent rolls.

Here is my big confession. I have always bought those magazines at the grocery store because many, many times I have said to myself that I really didn't need those magazines every month. I won't buy it this month but then I find myself at the checkout counter and there would be this lovely picture of tulips in a pale yellow vase and promises of five Quick and Easy suppers and quick and easy, it would end up in my cart. Rain, snow, or sleet; new babies, illness and surgery; four teenagers — nothing deterred me from those magazines.

When I retired, I made a huge concession to living out in the country. I got subscriptions for the two magazines. Maybe I thought I wouldn't be going to town every day or so. Or maybe I thought I wouldn't be spending as much time at the grocery store — no matter. It never occurred to me to stop buying the magazines.

Women's Day and *Family Circle* stayed relevant to me all the time I was raising children but I must admit they are not targeting retired women living in the woods. Many months, I don't find many articles that interest me but now I have a subscription that lasts for many years and each month, Tony, our faithful mail carrier, delivers them to my box.

Here is why I do this — at least I think it's the reason. I love opening the magazines and turning the pages to see what is in them and of course, it has a lot to do with my calendar interest. I get to see the decorations planned for each month and the recipes. Maybe this month, there will be the perfect recipe for a party I have planned. Or maybe this month, there will be an idea for a good way to organize something that I need to organize. I do think it feels like some kind of addiction. There is a rush as I open the first page and who knows what those glossy pages will hold for me this month? Perhaps the key to happiness lies buried in those colorful pages.

As I wrote that last line, it occurs to me that I maybe should get out more — get a life as my children say. But first, I think I'll get a cup of coffee and read this month's *Women's Day* and the new *Family Circle.*

Thank you, Holy God, for new ideas that give us a lift, hope that the next page we turn will be revelatory, time to sit down and have a cup of coffee, and traditions that are personal and life-giving. Amen.

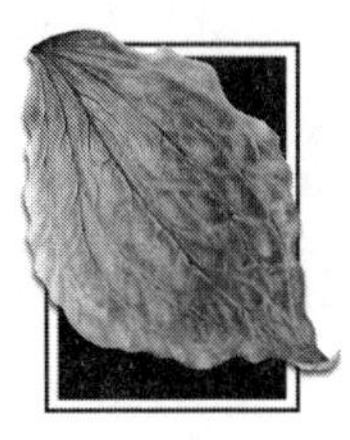

A Way With Words

My love of language started early. I love the English language. I am ashamed to admit that it is the only one I know. I have book learned several others, but English is the only one I can use.

As a child I remember reading *Johnny Tremain*. It was my first real grown-up book and there were many words I didn't know. But I got the sweep of the story and I remember wondering if I would ever be able to read a "hard" book and know all the words. It was that wonderment which has sent me on the word chase I still enjoy.

I love the English language and here is the wonder of it for me. All of us have more or less the same number of English words to work with, which is why it amazes me when ordinary people put ordinary words together in a way that I have never thought of — it delights me. Here are some examples:

- Shear Heaven – a beauty salon
- John McCain is between Barack and a hard place — an announcer on NPR on election day when Pennsylvania was declared for Obama
- Car Tunes — a call in request radio program during rush hour
- Purple Heys — a very attractive billboard advertising billboards
- Take it or Leave it — a consignment shop
- Shear Bliss — another beauty salon
- Logic Homes — this was the name of a store for log homes but I think it is a little too esoteric for cars driving by on the highway (not all of these are jewels)
- Kane is Able — sign on a furniture truck

- Prints Charming — headline for spring dresses
- Upper Crust — a café specializing in pies
- A Cut Above — yet another beauty salon
- Shore is Fine — the motto on a NJ license plate
- May "olive" your dreams come true — from an olive oil store
- The Bug Stops Here — an exterminator company
- Bank-A-Count — a payroll firm for small businesses
- Step In Time — a rehab center

Using words in different ways is fun and in addition to collecting phrases I also like to collect words themselves. The title of the last book, *Heading Home*, came about because "home" seemed to be such a prevalent theme as we retired. And the last year, I have been collecting "H" words, like heaven and hell, help and hurt, and holy and hope. I even put many of those words together for a weekend retreat.

I love the tricks that words can play. My friend was working on a crossword puzzle and had a word that started with "kn." "Oh," she said, "I guess that's a silent "K." Many "kn" words are important to me — words like knee, know, knit, knead, and kneel. But no one has ever accused me of being a silent Kay.

Thank you, Holy God, for minds that can use language, the delight of learning new words, patience as we learn a new language, and the human gift of languages all over the world. Amen.

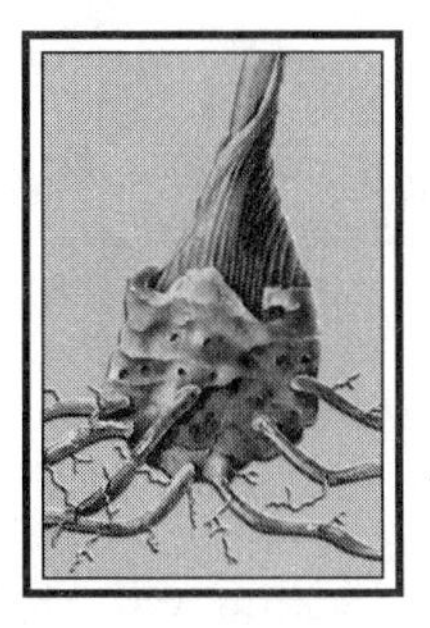

I Am A Writer

As mentioned earlier in the first chapter, I went to my first writer's conference in 2008. Actually it was called "A Festival of Faith and Writing" and it seemed a perfect fit for me. The registration bought me entry into dozens of workshops and lectures by "real" writers. It was stunning for me to see names on nametags of authors I had been reading for years. We all wore the same nametag — no differentiation between published, well-known authors and people like me. As the folks milled around that first afternoon, they introduced themselves to me. They were a friendly bunch. They asked me what I wrote and I awkwardly mumbled something about writing for our church publication. They smiled warmly. It was a very interesting collection of people. The women tended to be over 50 and dressed in flowing blouses and skirts in shades of tan and gold and olive green. They wore long dangling earrings. Dressed in my conservative Midwestern finest, I felt like the housemother to a grand bunch of hippies. Most of the men were also over 50 dressed in chinos and polo shirts, feet shod in walking shoes or an occasional Birkenstock sandal. I walked around trying to be nonchalant but truthfully, I could hardly contain myself when I saw "Mary Gordon" on a nametag or "Elizabeth Berg" or "Yann Martel" (*Life of Pi*). I could hardly keep myself from rushing up to them and gushing, "Oh I loved that part in your book when you..."

When I first got to the registration table, they asked me if I wanted to have an appointment with an agent. At first I politely declined but as the woman pressed me, I caved in and said yes. Two days later, I entered the room of a distinguished looking gentleman. He asked, "What are you working on now?" I told him that I was working on my third collection of essays. I could say that because by this time I had already attended the workshop by Brian Doyle and knew that I was an essayist.

More importantly, by this time it was getting a little easier to say, "I am a writer." I am not just someone who writes. I am a writer. I have always been a writer. I started early. I began writing four lines in a five-year diary when I was 14 years old. I have written my way through 53 years, using four short lines every night to describe, define, summarize, and nail down my day. It is one of the most consistent things of my life.

I went to a workshop led by Elizabeth Berg, author of many of my favorite novels. In the question and answer period, someone asked her what the best part of being a famous author was. This is how she answered: "I am going to tell you but you won't believe me. I do like the book tours, being interviewed by talk show hosts, and being treated like a celebrity. I am paid well. But the best part — the very best part is sitting myself down at my desk and writing — taking a blank page and filling it with characters and sentences and images." The best part is writing. That's true for me, too.

Thank you, Holy God, for the humility of really great people, clarity about who we are and what we can do, the thrill of a really good sentence, and for Jesus Christ as the Living Word. Amen.

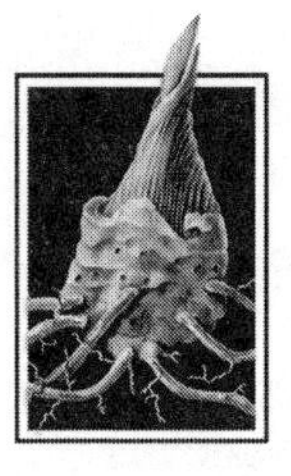

October

Orange pumpkins and black cats
Pungent smoke in the air
We dress up in costumes
And shout trick or treat
We gather ourselves together
And enjoy good things cooked in the oven

The Walk to Emmaus — Luke 24:13-18, 28-35

Now on that same day two of them were going to a village called Emmaus, about seven miles from Jerusalem, and talking with each other about all these things that had happened. While they were talking and discussing, Jesus himself came near and went with them, but their eyes were kept from recognizing him. And he said to them, "What are you discussing with each other while you walk along?" They stood still, looking sad. Then one of them, whose name was Cleopas, answered him, "Are you the only stranger in Jerusalem who does not know the things that have taken place there in these days?"

As they came near the village to which they were going, he walked ahead as if he were going on. But they urged him strongly, saying, "Stay with us, because it is almost evening and the day is now nearly over." So he went in to stay with them. When he was at the table with them, he took bread, blessed and broke it, and gave it to them. Then their eyes were opened, and they recognized him; and he vanished from their sight. They said to each other, "Were not our hearts burning within us while he was talking to us on the road, while he was opening the scriptures to us?" That same hour they got up and returned to Jerusalem; and they found the eleven and their companions gathered together. They were saying, "The Lord has risen indeed, and he has appeared to Simon!" Then they told what had happened on the road, and how he had been made known to them in the breaking of the bread.

One of the things we love to put in the oven is a really good meat loaf. This recipe from Nancy is exactly what October should taste like.

Pot Roast Meat Loaf

1 pound hamburger
⅔ cups evaporated milk
⅓ cup dry bread crumbs
¼ cup ketchup
1 teaspoon salt
2 teaspoons Worcestershire sauce
¼ teaspoon pepper

Mix together and shape into a loaf in the center of a 13 x 9 inch pan. Peel and slice ¼ inch thick, 3 potatoes, 3 onions, and 3 carrots. Toss into the pan around the meat loaf. Sprinkle all with salt and pepper and parsley flakes (optional). Cover with foil. Bake in a 375 degree oven about an hour. Uncover and bake another 10 minutes to brown the meat.

Thank you, Holy God, for the breaking of bread, the burning of a heart, the warmth of food and friends, and Jesus Christ, the Bread of the World. Amen.

AAUW Books

I sort books for the AAUW Book Sale as they are collected. They arrive in boxes and grocery bags and plastic sacks. They arrive in liquor boxes and large wooden boxes. Some of the bags are very predictable. They are packed tightly with paperbacks. For our purposes, there are few value judgments on paperbacks. A "racy" (my mother's term) romance novel with a bodice ripper cover lies cozily next to a dog-eared copy of "For Whom the Bell Tolls." They all go in the same category — paperback books.

The hard covers are easier to make judgments about. If they have clean covers and have been published in the last five years or so, they are "best sellers." Other hard covers go in categories, novels, non-fiction, etc.

I notice how people read non-fiction. Do they underline? (I don't write in books — *Heading Home*) Do they write in the margins? Do they write at the end or the beginning of the book, where there are blank pages?

As a writer, I always wondered how it would feel to see your work of art in a bargain books store. There it is — your life's work — five or six years of your life collected into one large amount of words and phrases and sentences. Your mother is proud — your children cheer. And then you walk into "Books for a Buck" and there is a huge stack of your precious books. They are piled waist-high on the floor. They are being sold for a dollar!

I now know how they feel. A couple of years ago, my friend was collecting and sorting books for the AAUW Book Sale and there it was — a copy of my first small book, *Of Season and Sparrows*. Ugh! Well, I guess it's better to resell it rather than throwing it into the paper recycling bin. At least maybe someone bought it for $.50 and took it home and maybe someone read it — all my hard work for $.50. Get over it, Kay.

I like opening the boxes that contain our good intentions. Here is a box of the healthy eating plan of someone, cookbooks and books of calorie counts and many different versions of diets, South Beach and Atkins and the Grapefruit Diet. They will be bought and taken home from our sale and become part of someone else's healthy eating plan.

The sorting goes quickly unless you start reading the inside covers. It breaks my heart to read "To Sarah for her Graduation from Aunt Lilah." The book doesn't look like it has ever been opened. You can make up the stories from reading the "personals."

"To my darling, Eva — this book made me think of us — as we used to be. Love, Frank."

"To Glen — I want to live in this small town. Your country mouse, Linda."

"To Joan — if wishes come true, this story would be me and you — love, Paul."

Little hopes and dreams, all there on the front page of a novel or a book of poetry. It's a little like eavesdropping into someone else's life. I try to be gentle.

Thank you, Holy God, for stories of our hearts in a book, good intentions to be well, good works on behalf of the community, and for a good book to fill our hours. Amen.

Singing The Blues

I went to an evening of music sponsored by our local college. I went because our friend, Greg, was playing in a jazz band as warm-up to the main event. The main event was the senior recital of a young songwriter, pianist, and blues singer. We loved the jazz band, then we watched as crew members moved a grand piano onto center stage. The young man, Dan, was accompanied on bass and woodwind by two members of the college music faculty. The theater dimmed and the spotlight rested on a tall, blond, young man, dressed in a doubled breasted black suit. He sat down at the piano and began to sing — his own songs, it turned out. His blond hair shone in the spotlight and he crooned one lovely song after another. After a particularly touching set, he stood at the mike and said, "I haven't lived long enough to be able to write about this much heartache." He smiled sheepishly and sat down at the piano and began another set. Of course, that is what every person in the audience over 40 was thinking. It was the acknowledgement and self-awareness that rang so true.

It might be my age (surely not) but I am always touched by the young people in my life. I am also aware we live in a world that is a little more dangerous than it was three decades ago when we were raising our children.

I was reminded of that when my friend called with a story. She and her daughter-in-law were shopping with three-year-old Matthew. They were in a huge warehouse store and one minute Matthew was standing quietly between them and the next he was gone. My friend started to go searching for Matthew, but Matthew's mother, Jackie began screaming "Secure the doors — lost child — secure the doors." The store personnel immediately took up their posts at all the doors and then all joined in, calling Matthew's name. He was found, safe and sound, in about 15 minutes.

To be honest, mothers of my generation were not taught to scream and shout for the doors to be locked, just in case someone had abducted their child. No one thought of that when our children were lost. We think of that now. So it is even more of a blessing when I witness the courage of young families.

There is a young family in our church and one morning I watched the father as he helped his two children out of their boots and winter coats. As they started up the stairs to their Sunday school class, he patted his son on the back and said, "Go and learn something good about Jesus."

And I love being in worship with all the little wiggly ones. I love seeing them come to the front of the church for the children's chat with our pastor, Tammie. And I love hearing the sweet little voice that sits behind me in the pew as we pray the Lord's Prayer. She is just a few words behind. I am grateful and I am a rich woman surrounded by young people who fill me with hope.

Thank you, Holy God, for people who come to look for us when we are lost, young families who are raising good children in a dangerous world, the hope children bring to the world, and anyone who still seeks the Good News of Jesus. Amen.

Web Of Prayer

Sometimes, at a church conference, a speaker will say one thing that makes you glad you came. That happened to me. In the midst of many presentations, a speaker said something like this, "Women's greatest fear is abandonment and men's greatest fear is helplessness."

That bit about helplessness sent me off on a quest to uncover the word, "help." I began playing with the word and all its nuances. Help — helpless, helpful, needing help, asking for help. The image of HELP being spelled out in coconuts on a sandy beach kept running through my head. I thought back to the time that I got locked in a bathroom in Germany and found myself calling for help, quietly at first, embarrassed and then louder as the reality of my situation hit me. I hollered "help" and someone came and helped me. Helping someone is a very good thing. Someone has a need and asks us for help and we can do it. Whether that is getting our tractor and pulling someone out of the ditch or picking up a child after school or editing a resume, we like being thought of as people who help others. It is a much better feeling than needing help ourselves and trying to find the courage to ask for it.

Sometimes we are asked to help with things that we can't fix, like a broken heart or a broken body. Unless we are physicians, we usually can't help. But our faith offers something we can always do. We can hold a person in our thoughts. We can hold a person in prayer. And we do. But we might think that we should do more.

We have a friend who lost her husband. She was left with a five-year-old daughter. At the memorial service, she thanked everyone for coming. She said, "Your prayers were so appreciated. They did not change anything, but they did make a net under me. And though I bounced a little, like on a trampoline, I did not fall." She did not fall because that web of prayer and love and concern became for her, almost tangible.

A participant in one of my retreats shared this insight. When we do something for someone to help, we hear ourselves saying, "Oh, it was the least I could do." It's a funny phrase — like I made a list of all the things I could do and did the one that cost me the least trouble. We probably should say, "oh, it was the most I could do." And after you have made a list of all the things you could do, prayer should be at the top of the list. Prayer is often the most we can do. It is a way that we can help.

Anne Lamotte says there are only two prayers — "Help me, help me" and "Thank you, thank you." So now that I have explored the topic of helplessness, perhaps I should move on to abandonment. Help!

Thank you, Holy God, for people who know how to help, the willingness to ask for help when we need it, the web of prayer that holds us, and for the mercy you grant when we call to you for help. Amen.

November

This month is gray and black and white
After six months of green
The trees are now bare and stark
It is now consistently cold
No chance of reprieve
And we look for warmth amidst the gray
So nature sends us Thanksgiving
And we warm ourselves with
Gratefulness and family
And friends around the table

The Widow's Offering — Mark 12:41-44

He sat down opposite the treasury, and watched the crowd putting money into the treasury. Many rich people put in large sums. A poor widow came and put in two small copper coins, which are worth a penny. Then he called his disciples and said to them, "Truly I tell you, this poor widow has put in more than all those who are contributing to the treasury. For all of them have contributed out of their abundance; but she out of her poverty has put in everything she had, all she had to live on."

There is one recipe in our family that appears at every gathering. It is a church recipe from way back in the 1980s when we served congregations in Indiana. Every first Sunday of the month, one of the congregations had a Pitch-In after worship. Pitch-in is Hoosier for Potluck or Covered Dish Dinner. At each Pitch-In there were congregational favorites. Our children looked forward to the wonderful assortment of jello salads, many of which contained fruit and lots of whipped cream and marshmallows. One dear woman brought a huge pan of pork chops every month. And then there was the Corn Casserole, brought by Fran. She wrote out the recipe for me calling it corn casserole but our family has always called it scalloped corn. Whatever you call it, it is very good.

Scalloped Corn (Corn Casserole)

1 can cream style corn (about 15 ounces)
1 can whole kernel corn (about 15 ounces)
1 package Jiffy Corn Muffin Mix (the one that makes 6 corn muffins)
1 egg
1 cup sour cream
½ - 1 tablespoon of garlic powder
¼ cup of butter, cut into pats and laid on top of mixture

You can put all the ingredients in a casserole and mix it up right in there. I have never used the garlic powder but you could try it both ways and see which way your family likes it best.

You bake this in a 350 degree oven for about an hour or until the middle doesn't jiggle.

Thank you, Holy God, for poor widows who give all they have, generosity in the things we give, autumn days and the joy of holidays, and any time that we can gather and give thanks. Amen.

A Fool-Proof Thanksgiving Dinner

Many years ago when our girls were setting up housekeeping, I sent them a little memo to help them prepare their first Thanksgiving Dinner consisting of:

Roast turkey
Mashed potatoes and gravy
Dressing (or stuffing as we call it)
Cranberry sauce and a vegetable
Pumpkin pie with whipped cream

For the turkey: buy a frozen turkey about 10 – 12 pounds. It usually goes on sale at this time of year. I have enclosed a roasting bag. You will need a pan big enough for the turkey, with sides on it but if you don't have one, you can buy a foil one.

Thaw the turkey. This takes a long time. Put it in the sink with water covering it until it thaws. There are icky things inside the turkey (both ends sometimes) — just throw those away.

I always follow directions and put a little flour in the bottom of the bag and make the tiny slits for the steam to get out. Tie him (or her) up with the enclosed tie — it was folded in the plastic bag — it may now be on the floor. Getting the turkey into the bag is a two-person job. The chart will tell you how long to cook it. I usually leave it in for another 30 minutes just for good measure.

When the time is up, your turkey should be golden brown. Ignore all the juice in the bottom of the bag unless you are going to make your own gravy (that would require another page of instructions, not included here). Well, don't exactly ignore it. When the turkey is taken out, carefully dispose of the whole bag with the juice. Don't put it down the drain. That would be bad.

Mashed potatoes — you could buy potatoes, peel them, cook them, mash them with a little milk, salt, and butter OR you could use the enclosed coupon to buy some instant ones — your choice.

Since you have already gotten rid of the juice in the bag, just prepare the gravy from the handy mix I have also included.

Speaking of mixes, I have included an article about the best stuffing mixes so buy a package and prepare it according to the directions.

You will need cranberry sauce in a can, if you really want to have an "authentic" American Thanksgiving dinner. And we want you to support the cranberry industry in central Wisconsin.

Frozen peas or broccoli are good with turkey — or you could just make a plate of raw veggies to nibble on.

While you are in the freezer section, pick up a package of pie crust. You will need a pie plate but they also come in foil. The pumpkin pie mix requires a can of evaporated milk and a couple of eggs — the recipe is on the can. Or you can just buy a pumpkin pie, but really a pumpkin pie is the easiest thing to make. Of course, you will need whipped cream for the top — your father thinks that is the reason people eat pumpkin pie.

When the food is prepared, take a picture of your family around the table and thank God for each other.

Thank you, Holy God, for the days we set aside to be thankful, for shortcuts and cooking from scratch, generations of family cooks, and for family and friends gathered around the table. Amen.

Cancer Survivors Day

Last May I was asked to be the keynote speaker at our local hospital's Cancer Survivors Day. I hadn't ever thought of myself as a cancer survivor but I have had a couple of bouts of cancer and I am still surviving and I am grateful. I have learned a little bit about cancer over the years.

This is what I know:

God doesn't give cancer to us to punish us, to test us, or to make us better people. Cancer comes to us (an equal opportunity disease) because we live in a toxic world   not the world God intended for us but here it is and here we are. Our being good or bad people has nothing to do with our getting cancer. I will die some day, from cancer or from something else and that is true for everyone. Since Frances often comes to me when I am a little concerned about something, she tells the next story.

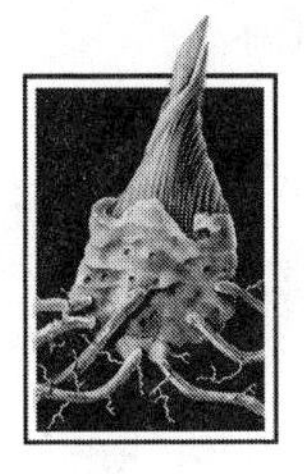

Frances Beside Herself

The room is blue, that Wedgwood blue designed to be calming in a decorative way. Bookshelves, blue bookshelves line one wall. There aren't many books. The shelves are used for other objects and are clearly in place to convey to occupants that this is an ordinary room. But this is no ordinary room.

Frances sits on the sculpted blue plastic chair with her purse at her side and her appointment book on her lap. She centers herself in the chair, smiling as she remembers her friend telling a story about Catholic school. "You had to sit right in the middle of the chair so that your guardian angels would have room to sit on each side of you," her friend had said. "Better move your purse," she said to herself. She patted her appointed book for comfort. It was something to hang onto that was ordinary and commonplace.

Frances had her speech ready. She had made up her mind. After six weeks of testing, she would agree to no more tests. She had been cooperative and compliant all this time, but no more. This was becoming embarrassing. So much time and so much money and all for nothing. Every test came flying back with the news that everything was fine. So the story today would be that Frances was ready to get on with her life. The little problem would go away. It seemed to have gone away already. It was all just stress. "Everything is always just stress," Frances thought. It was like saying, it was all just breathing, as if one could live without air or anxiety. But if it was stress, changes had been made. There would be no more tests.

Frances felt like a schoolgirl waiting for the principal to come in. She watched the door. It opened and in walked the doctor. She was tall and slim and carried a file, her file, Frances guessed. She sat down on the little rolling stool, a milking stool on wheels and opened the file. She stared intently at the words inside and did not look at

Frances. Frances waited for her chance to begin the conversation and tell the doctor how things were going to be, to tell the doctor her decision that there would be no more tests.

Frances started to speak but before the words came out, the doctor began to speak, "We've found a mass but it's low grade and..." The doctor's mouth kept moving. She was still talking but Frances couldn't hear. She stared at the way the doctor's lips kept forming words. The words made sounds, but they were unreliable sounds, sounds that lacked meaning. A voice broke into the sounds and Frances was surprised to hear her own voice ask, "What does low grade mean?"

The doctor began speaking again, this time more slowly, but the words once again became sounds, slower sounds but still unintelligible. The doctor continued to speak in this strange, low, guttural language while she directed Frances up on the examining table. As she obediently climbed up on the crinkly white paper, Frances felt her mind veering off somewhere so she wouldn't have to hear the rest of the doctor's words. She had a tumor, a mass. What a funny word — mass. "The mass has ended. Let us go in peace." The blessing came to her from somewhere. It felt comforting. It felt hopeful. Her mind kept picking at it though, until it didn't feel so hopeful any more. Frances tuned back in for a moment, straining to decipher the incomprehensible sounds. The doctor efficiently continued, "I'll have my staff get going on the paperwork and make the appointment with the hospital. Do you have any questions?" Frances was sure she did have questions but she couldn't get her brain and mouth to work well enough together to form any words. Compliantly, she walked out of the office. She was directed to another desk and Frances began to flip through the days and weeks of her appointment book. The dates and tiny words of classes and meetings blurred as she studied September. A day was chosen.

Back at work, it was Frances who went into several offices and calmly made arrangements. It looked like Frances, at least on the outside but on the inside, Frances watched with interest as this very controlled woman told folks of the surgery and of the tumor. She watched this woman leave the building and walk to her office. Frances was beside herself. She sat down at her familiar desk, with the smiling picture of her family.

It was then that one question loomed up from her stomach. Like bile, like vomit, like some evil being, it pushed itself up from her solar plexus into her throat. She could taste it. She could taste the question. “No, she would have said the word,” whispered Francis. She had not heard the word. “This is a mistake.”

Frances began to shake. She opened the appointment book and there was the paper with the time of surgery and carefully clipped on the top, the doctor’s card. After several false starts, she dialed the number. Soon she was speaking to the cheery nurse. “This is Frances. I was just in to see the doctor and I have a question that I didn’t think to ask.” Frances forced herself to be breezy, to keep it light, although she was sure that the nurse would be able to hear her heart pounding wildly over the telephone.

Then the question rose from that deep place within her. “Do I have cancer?” The cheery nurse chirped, yes.

Thank you, Holy God, for strength when we get bad news, the ability to cope and stand it, and the hope when there doesn’t seem to be any; for doctors and researchers; the growth that can come from adversity; knowing the difference between curing and healing; and the common thread we feel in our humanity. Amen.

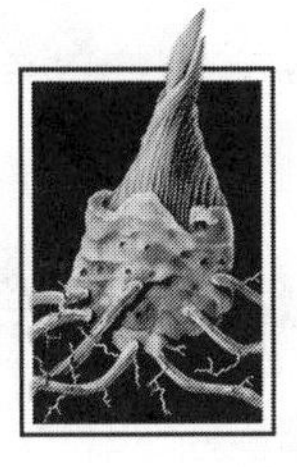

December

Red and green and gold and silver
Some white for a snowflake or two
December is in a rush heading for the 25th
We count the days on the Advent calendar
We turn the pages of the catalogs
We think of friends and family
And sometimes send them cards
And we praise God and are amazed
At the Good News of the birth of Jesus Christ

The Birth of Jesus — Luke 2:1-20

In those days a decree went out from Emperor Augustus that all the world should be registered. This was the first registration and was taken while Quirinius was governor of Syria. All went to their own towns to be registered. Joseph also went from the town of Nazareth in Galilee to Judea, to the city of David called Bethlehem, because he was descended from the house and family of David. He went to be registered with Mary, to whom he was engaged and who was expecting a child. While they were there, the time came for her to deliver her child. And she gave birth to her firstborn son and wrapped him in bands of cloth, and laid him in a manger, because there was no place for them in the inn.

In that region there were shepherds living in the fields, keeping watch over their flock by night. Then an angel of the Lord stood before them, and the glory of the Lord shone around them, and they were terrified. But the angel said to them, "Do not be afraid; for see — I am bringing you good news of great joy for all the people: to you is born this day in the city of David a Savior, who is the Messiah, the Lord. This will be a sign for you: you will find a child wrapped in bands of cloth and lying in a manger." And suddenly there was with the angel a multitude of the heavenly host, praising God and saying, "Glory to God in the highest heaven, and on earth peace among those whom he favors!"

When the angels had left them and gone into heaven, the shepherds said to one another, "Let us go now to Bethlehem and see this thing that has taken place, which the Lord has made known to us." So they went with haste and found Mary and Joseph and the child lying in the manger. When they saw this, they made known what had been told them about this child; and all who heard it were amazed at what the shepherds told them. But Mary treasured all these words and pondered them in her heart. The shepherds returned, glorifying and praising God for all they had heard and seen, as it had been told them.

Chicken Spread

This recipe is printed on an old piece of newspaper from decades ago. It was my mother's favorite food.

1 can (5 ounces) chunky chicken, undrained
1 package (8 ounces) cream cheese at room temperature
1 teaspoon dehydrated minced onion
1 tablespoon soy sauce

Cream together and serve on crackers. It is best served at room temperature.

Thank you, Holy God, for the delicious joy of Christmas, gifts given and gifts received, generosity displayed, and for the gift of Jesus Christ. Amen.

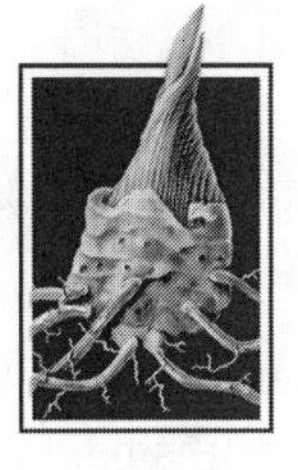

I'M A GRANDMA

There are Cheerios stuck to the breakfast nook. There is a tiny tiara from the Bratz doll and old go-go boots from the vintage thirty year-old Barbie dolls. Video cameras intermingle with the iPods and hi-tech phones sitting alongside Grandma's 35 mm camera that still uses "real" film. The suitcase lies open at the bottom of the stairs, with dress-ups spilling out, scarves and necklaces (or neckolaces, as Maddie calls them) and hats and pieces of cloth to wrap up in. Thirty year-old Fisher Price people stand alongside fluorescent "My Little Ponies." Old fashioned fairy tale books lay alongside 2007 TV personalities — Dora the Explorer and SpongeBob SquarePants.

This is Christmas — two daughters, two son-in-laws, and three grandgirls in one small woods home. Our daughters are reliving their childhood one toy at a time. Here is the wind-up toy that shows nursery rhymes going around playing some cheery song. It still plays. It was the high tech toy that lulled our girls to sleep almost 40 years ago. Now our granddaughters are soothed to sleep with a small, personal DVD playing "Mickey's Best Christmas."

I look at the handprints on the windows and the glass door between the cabin and the house, on the wall going down the stairs and I know I will not be able to wash them off for a very long time. They are as precious as the hands that made them.

...I have played games with my children, held sleepy girls, played games with the grandgirls.

...I have cooked and sat at the table looking at our family busily eating.

...I have knit scarves for the women and girls glad to have something to do with my hands as the girls play.

…I have cleaned up spilled juice, crushed cookies, and joined with everyone else to wash the endless cups and glasses.

…I have sat quietly in my chair and watched the activity whirling around me, children dancing and singing.

…I have mouthed a silent thank you for my family, imperfect and flawed but doing the best we can.

…I have tried to remain an unanxious presence during occasional crises, meltdowns, and sharp words.

…I have smiled to myself at my children's children — at Maddie, having a spell on the couch. "Maddie, do you want to come and play with your cousins?" "Not yet — I'm not done crying."

…I have laughed — oh — how I have laughed at silly girls dressed up and posing — at silly grownups wearing hats and making faces.

…I am a grandma never getting enough hugs or sticky kisses or secrets.

…I am a lucky woman.

…I am a grandma.

…I am tired!

Thank you, Holy God, for hearts filled to overflowing, silly children and silly grownups, moments to remember, handprints on the wall, and the time of my life. Amen.

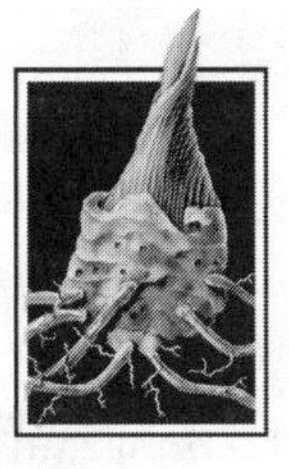

CHRISTMAS EVE

Lights shone brightly from the small farmhouse. The voices of children laughing came across the night air as the family made its way to the car. Large snowflakes fell as the car made its way down the narrow snowplowed driveway on the way to the small country church for the Christmas Eve service.

A tall, lanky farmer stood in the doorway shaking his head. Hmph! Anyone would be crazy to start out in a blizzard. Well, he'd just use the time to enjoy a cup of coffee and the quiet of his old farmhouse. Suddenly he was jolted out of his chair by a thud. Running to the window, he saw what had happened. A small sparrow had mistakenly tried to seek shelter in the warmth of the house and had crashed into the window. He could see the small bird lying in the snow.

Birds had flown into the window before and he had watched the stunned birds slowly regain their ability to fly. Tonight however, the small bird lay perfectly still.

He put on his big parka and headed around to the front of the house. Once there, he could see that this small bird wasn't a solitary traveler. Huddled in the small bushes by the house were several more sparrows, struggling to hold themselves fast to the branches. Looking around to make sure that no one was watching, he bent down and carefully picked up the bird in a mittened hand and made his way to the dimly lit barn. He laid the bird on a pile of clean hay and looked up into the dark corner of the hayloft.

Gentle fluttering in the darkness told him that many small creatures had already found shelter and he thought of those still out in the storm. He reached for an old lantern and lighting it, he headed out into the night again. He would try to get those birds to safety. Though it sounded foolish, perhaps in the magic of Christmas Eve, they would understand and follow him.

He started for the barn again saying foolish things like, "Here, birdie! Come with me, birdie." But not a bird moved to follow him.

Trudging back to the barn, he had another idea. He grabbed the sack of birdfeed from just inside the door and hurried back to the window. He poured out a trail of seed leading to the barn. His hopes soared as a few of the more brave souls hopped down to grab a few seeds but the trail was soon obliterated by the snow. If only he could find a way to lead them out of the storm. He whispered "If only I could become one of them for just a moment or two, I could show them the way out of the storm. I could save them."

The old man lifted himself from the mound of snow and started back to the house. Once inside, the old man stood before the fire warming himself when he felt a prayer beginning. It was a simple prayer and it ended with thanks, for the car had turned into the driveway bringing his family home safely.

For God loved the world so much that God had come to the world to bring all people out of the storm. God had despaired of trying to save it until God became a man and could show the way. This was the night of the birth of that God-man, Jesus Christ, born in a manger.

Thank you, Holy God, for the people who lead us out of darkness, warm cups of coffee on a cold night, for the love that shows us the way, and for your love that saves us. Amen.